MW00587925

SCHOOL OF DARKNESS

BELLA V. DODD

SCHOOL
OF DARKNESS

 Angelico Press

Angelico Press reprint edition, 2017
This Angelico Press edition is a republication
of the work originally published by
P. J. Kenedy & Sons, New York, 1954

For information, address:
Angelico Press
4709 Briar Knoll Dr.
Kettering, OH 45429
info@angelicopress.com

978-1-62138-292-8 (pb)
978-1-62138-293-5 (cloth)

Cover Design: Michael Schrauzer

And in the School of Darkness learn
What mean
"The things unseen."

JOHN BANISTER TABB

CHAPTER ONE

I WAS BORN in southern Italy on a farm that had been in my mother's family for generations. But I was really an American born on Italian soil as the result of a series of accidents, and it was also an accident which kept me in Italy until I was almost six years old. Not until years afterward did I learn that one reason my mother had left me there was in the hope that someday she could persuade her husband, in New York with her other children, to return with them to Italy. To her that farm near Potenza was home. But she was never able to persuade them of that, for America was the place of their choice.

My mother had been left a widow when the youngest of her nine children was still a baby. With the help of the older children she ran the farm. If Rocco Visono had not come to Potenza from his home in Lugano no doubt she would have remained there the rest of her life.

But Rocco fell in love with Teresa Marsica who, despite her nine children and a life of work, was still attractive, with bright, dark eyes and lively ways. Rocco had come to visit a sister married to a petty government official and met Teresa in the nearby village of Picerno. A stonemason by trade, he found work in Potenza while Teresa was making up her mind. She was almost persuaded but hesitated when she learned that he planned to go to New York. It took a long time to get her to agree to that. She would look at her rich soil that grew good lettuce and beans. This had been her father's farm and her grandfather's and his father's. How could she give it up and cross the Atlantic to uncertainty, and perhaps have no land there to cherish and work?

But the quiet, blue-eyed suitor was persistent. The children were on his side, too, eager to go to America, for Rocco had told them glowing stories of the life there, of the freedom and the chance to get rich. They argued and pleaded with their mother until she gave in.

The three oldest boys were to go with their father-elect, and my mother and the others were to join them later. I say "elect" purposely, for Teresa, for reasons of her own, had insisted that she would not marry him until she arrived in America. Having lost all the rest of the issues, he had to yield on this also, and the four left for the United States.

From East Harlem they sent enthusiastic reports. There were many Italians living there; it was like a colony of home people; she must come quickly. So Teresa accepted the inevitable. She said good-by to her neighbors and her beloved fields, to the house that had sheltered her all her life and in which all her children had been born. She put the farm in the charge of a relative for she could not bear to sell it. She might come back someday. With six children she sailed for the new home.

The three older boys and Rocco took her in triumph to their five-room flat on 108th Street. Teresa was happy to

2

see them again, but she looked with dismay at the honey-comb of rooms. She was only partly comforted when her sister, Maria Antonia, who had been in America for some time, came to welcome her.

In January 1904 Rocco Visono and Teresa Marsica were married in the Church of St. Lucy in East Harlem. It was perhaps on that day she felt most homesick of all, for a memory came to her when she heard the words of the priest — a recollection of the past, of Fidelia, her mother, and Severio, her father, and the farm workers and herself and her brothers and sisters, all kneeling together at family prayer in the big living room of the Picerno farmhouse.

Several months later a letter came from Italy telling Teresa that there was trouble with the management of her property. At this news she persuaded Rocco that she must go back to adjust matters, perhaps rent the farm to responsible people, or even — this was his suggestion — sell it outright.

It was not until she was on the high seas that Teresa realized she was pregnant. She was dismayed. The business in Italy might take months and the baby might be born there.

The affairs of the farm took longer than she expected. In October of 1904 I was born in Picerno and baptized Maria Assunta Isabella. With my father's approval Teresa decided to return to the United States and leave me in charge of a foster mother. She hoped to return within a year, but it was five years before she saw me again. I was almost six years old when I saw my father and brothers and sister for the first time.

The woman who became my foster mother and wet nurse was the wife of a shepherd in Avialano. Her own baby had died and she was happy to have me. For five years I lived with these simple people. Though there was little luxury in the small stone house, I received loving care from both my foster parents. I remember them and my memories go back to my third year. Mamarella was a good woman and I was greatly devoted to her. But it was to her husband, Taddeo, that my deepest love went. There was no other child in the family and to me he gave all his parental affection.

I remember their home with the fireplace, the table drawn up before it for supper, I in Taddeo's arms, his big shepherd's coat around me. In later days, when life was difficult, I often wished I were again the little child who sat there snug in the protecting love about her.

My mother sent money regularly, and gave my foster parents more comforts than the small wages of Taddeo could provide. Time and again Mamarella tried to make of Taddeo something more than a hill shepherd. She disliked his being away from home in the winter, but in that mountainous part of Italy it was cold in the winter; so the sheep were driven to the warmer Apulia where the grazing was better.

Even in the summer Taddeo often stayed all night in the hills. Then Mamarella and I went to him carrying food and blankets so that we, too, might sleep in the open. While husband and wife talked, I would wander off for flowers and butterflies. I remember running from one hilltop to another. My eager fingers stretched upward, for the sky seemed so close I thought I could touch it. I would come back tired to find Mamarella knitting and Taddeo whittling a new pair of wooden shoes for me. Not until just before I left for America did I wear a pair of leather shoes.

Taddeo would give me warm milk from his sheep and try to explain to me about the sky. Once he said: "Never mind, little one. Perhaps someday you will touch the sky. Perhaps!"

4

Then he would tell me stories about the stars, and I almost believed that they belonged to him and that he could move them in the heavens. I would fall asleep wrapped in a blanket. When I awoke I would find myself in my own bed back at our house on the edge of the village.

I have vague memories of the things of religion. I remember being carried on Taddeo's shoulders on a pilgrimage with many people walking through a deep forest several days and nights to some shrine. It must have been spring for the woods were carpeted with violets. I have never since seen blue wood violets without hearing in my mind the hum of prayers said together by many people.

One of the children told me about a place called purgatory. She said that if you let the bishop put salt on your tongue and water on your forehead you got into heaven, and that if it were not done you stayed in purgatory for years and years. I took this matter to Taddeo and for once he was not reassuring. Purgatory was a gray place, he said, with no trees and no hills, but he said he would be there with me.

He talked to Mamarella, and she said though I was young she was going to have me confirmed because the bishop was coming to our town to perform the ceremony. This called for great preparations. I had a new red dress with a high neck made "princess style." I was to have my first pair of leather shoes.

When the great day came I was at church early. It was still almost empty save for the restless group of children awaiting confirmation. The few seats in the big church were placed toward the altar. You did not sit in these for they were for the gentry of the town. Everyone else knelt on the stone floor.

I knelt, too, and looked around me at the statues. I had a favorite among them: St. Anthony, with the tender smile and the Christ Child on his arm. Taddeo told me that St. Anthony would watch over me and keep me from evil; and that if I lost something St. Anthony would help find it.

One evening at supper we heard hurried footfalls and an excited voice calling:

"*Una lettera d'America!*"

"Maybe it's from my mother," I said, "and there will be money in it for Mamarella."

When she opened it I saw only a very little letter and no money at all. No one told me what the letter was about.

Weeks later I was alone in the house, close by the fire. February was cold that year. Taddeo was in Apulia and would not be back for some time. Mamarella had gone to the village fountain for drinking water.

I heard strange steps on the cobblestones. The door opened and there stood a tall, dark woman in a heavy coat who looked at me and without a word put her arms around me and hugged me. Then she took off her veil and I saw she had thick black hair, a little gray, but soft and wavy.

I looked at her with amazement. "Who are you?" I asked.

She answered me in Italian, but it sounded different from that of our village. "I'm a friend of the people who live here. Where is the shepherd?"

"He isn't here. He's in Apulia."

"Do you like him?"

"I love him better than anyone in the world. I love him all the time." I stared at her and wondered why she should ask such questions.

"Of course you do," she said soothingly. "Come over here and sit on my lap while I tell you a story. But first, do you love him better than your own mother?"

"Of course I do. I don't even know my own mother."

The strange lady smiled at me. "Listen, dear, I had a

little girl myself once." As I listened I began to feel uneasy. "I had to go away to a strange land where I couldn't take care of her and so I found a good kind man who said he would. His name was Taddeo."

"Taddeo?" Suddenly I understood and slipped from the woman's lap. "You're my real mother."

She stroked my hair and said, "I have come all the way from America for my baby girl and I hoped she would love me."

Something in her voice won me over. I went to her and put my arms around her neck and so we sat until Mamarella came in. I was half asleep and remembered only saying, "This is my mother, my real mother. You have to love your mother."

She went away again that evening, but she said she would be back in a week or else send for me. She promised to take me with her to America.

Now all was feverish preparation. Word was sent to Taddeo and he sent back word that he would be home before I left. For me that last week was one of triumph among my playmates.

"Did she bring you presents?" the children asked. "Will you go in the coach to Potenza?"

"The houses in America are made of glass," said another child. "No one is poor there. Everyone is happy."

"And they eat macaroni every day," piped another. This even I knew would be a wonderful thing, for to eat macaroni every day was the essence of plutocracy to children whose chief diet was beans and polenta.

"And will you come back?" someone asked.

Somehow this was the first time I had actually thought of going away and I felt a little shaken, but I answered boldly, "Of course I will, and someday I'll take you all with me to America."

No further word had come from Taddeo on the eve of my departure to join my mother. Mamarella had prepared a wonderful supper of *pasta arricata,* and nuts and squids stuffed with raisins. There was sweet white wine. It was like *carnevale.* We waited for Taddeo but when he did not come, we sat down and ate in silence. Then we cleared the table. I sat with my head against Mamarella's chair. She was crying, but she stopped when she saw that I was crying, too. She took me in her arms and sang to me — a song about the saints.

Still Taddeo did not come. I feared I would never see him again. I tried to picture exactly how he had looked so I would always remember him.

When the fire was embers, Mamarella put ashes over it and we went to bed; but I could not sleep. Suddenly I heard what I had been listening for — heavy steps on the cobblestones. When the door opened I was in his arms. My feet were cold and he took off his muffler and wound it round them and rubbed them.

Mamarella came in and poked up the fire and said to me sharply, *"Non far mosso,"* and began warming polenta. I sat still in his arms while Taddeo talked to us about his trip home.

"I traveled half the night and had no idea it would be so cold in Avialano," he said. He must get to the sheep-fold in the valley right away, he said, for he had left the sheep in charge of Filippi. He could stay only an hour with us.

"St. Anthony brought me," he told me. "He helped get me here in time. Don't ever forget he will help you get where you ought to go and find what you lose."

I paid little attention to his words. I was happy to sit by the fire and watch him eat polenta and dip bread into the red wine.

8

Then he rose, put on his long cloak, and tied the muffler around his neck. "This muffler is too thin to be of much use any more. Listen, child, will you send me a new one from America?"

My eyes filled with tears. He kissed me. "There, *carina*, someday you will come back," he said reassuringly. "And you are going now to a fine home where you will be *una signorina* and have silk dresses and maybe *two* pairs of leather shoes."

"I don't want to go," I cried in panic. "I won't go! I won't!"

He held me until I stopped sobbing and then he said, "Now I must really go. *Addio, carina*," and he handed me over to Mamarella and hurried from the house. I struggled free and ran after him. I had no shawl and my dress flew in the wind. I kept calling, "Taddeo! Taddeo!" I ran down the street till I came to the piazza and I could see Taddeo and Filippi driving the sheep ahead of them. It was bitter cold and the ground was icy.

I called Taddeo again and again. I had put on my first pair of leather shoes to show to him and the untied laces made me stumble; the hard leather hurt my feet. I lay in the snow and sobbed. There Mamarella found me and took me home and put me between hot blankets. She stayed with me until I fell asleep.

Next day I was dressed in my red confirmation dress which was to have been saved to wear on the feast of the Virgin and *carnevale*. My hair was carefully combed. The leather shoes were laced around my ankles. Mamarella brought out her wedding box and drew from it a white silk kerchief. "I wore it when I was a girl," she said, as she folded it in a triangle and tied it under my chin. Then we went to the coach which was waiting to take me away.

"*Madonna, questa creatura e tutti occhi*," said the coachman when he saw his smaller passenger. Mamarella and I sat in the coach in silence and watched the desolate mountain scenery and the snowdrifts banked along the road. Finally, numb with cold, we reached the railroad station in Potenza. Mamarella put me on the train and kissed me. I could not cry for all the feeling was drained from me. Then I was alone on a train with strangers and on my way to Naples where my mother was to meet me.

It was the first time I had ever been on a train but I did not find it strange. I looked out of the window at the changing landscape. After awhile there were no snow and no mountains, only grass and plains, with olive trees here and there. Once I saw a flock of white sheep with a shepherd, and I thought of Taddeo. But Taddeo was now far behind, and I was alone. I had left everything I knew and was going into the unknown.

The compartment in which I rode was almost empty. The conductor had promised Mamarella that he would take care of me. Finally, as I sat on the wooden bench, I fell asleep, leaning against my bundle of clothes, exhausted by the strange movement of the train.

It was night when the train pulled into Naples. The conductor came in and picked up my bundle. *"Viene subito,"* he said, and I followed him to the platform. And there was my mother looking anxiously for me. She was tall and straight and reassuring. I waved excitedly to her and it made me happy to see her warm smile as she ran toward me.

I was frightened by what I saw of Naples. There were beggars whining and wheedling in the name of St. Rocco. There were dirty children in the streets. There was noise and confusion. I wanted to fly back to our quiet little village, where the people were poor, but clean and proud.

I was glad when the next day we sailed for America.

10

CHAPTER TWO

THE REASON my mother had not returned to Italy for me for five long years, my father later explained, was because there had been a terrible depression in America. It had been impossible for him to raise the money for Mother to make the trip, and a small child could not travel alone. I had been shy in meeting my father. He was blond, blue-eyed, and reserved, the opposite of Mother. But despite his quiet, undemonstrative manner I felt that he loved me. He was kind and he made a pet of me.

There were only four children at home now; the rest had married and had homes of their own. They came to see the new sister and made a big fuss over me. But they all made fun of my best dress — my red confirmation dress which every child in Avialano had admired. They laughed at me and insisted I be rushed to a store to buy an American dress. With great reluctance I put away the beautiful red princess dress and with it the last of my Italian years. And I turned with zeal to the task of becoming an American child.

The three brothers still at home were kind enough, but they had their own interests which were certainly not those of a six-year-old girl and one who could speak no English. But my seventeen-year-old sister, Caterina, called by the American name of Katie, took me in hand. She was a tall, slim, beautiful girl with big gray eyes. She was kind and gentle. She did not like the name I was called by — Maria Assunta — and when she learned that I had been baptized with another name — Isabella — she insisted on calling me Bella.

Katie took me to school. She had made up her mind I was a smart little thing and so she got me in a grade ahead by saying I was born in 1902 instead of two years later. In those earlier educational days she had no difficulty in having me enrolled in the second grade. For a few days I was pursued by cries of "wop, wop," but I paid no attention to them. I did not know what they meant and by the time I did I had been accepted as a leader in my class.

I liked going and coming from school, especially wandering along and staring at the merchandise piled up on barrows right in the street. You could buy fruit and peppers and sweets and even dress goods and hats there. I liked to watch the pigeons in the street strutting about in their gray and rose coats and silver wings.

My mother did not share my delight in the city. "If we lived in the country!" she would remark sometimes. Only later I learned how much she hated the dirty streets, the gossip of her neighbors, the narrow flat. There were parks, of course, but they made her even more homesick for the open fields.

Mother was a competent woman. She could do a prodigious amount of work and never looked tired or bedraggled. She quickly established a routine of work and play for me. She tried to help me learn English though her own was far from good. She would point to a calendar and repeat each month and day in her curious, soft English and I would repeat the words after her. She would then take the broom and point out the hours and minutes on the old-fashioned kitchen clock, and again I would repeat what she said.

I think one reason for these educational efforts was that she wanted to keep me busy after school for she would not let me spend time in the city streets. She taught me to sew and crochet; sometimes she would take a crochet needle and coarse thread and show me simple stitches. "Someday you will crochet a bridal spread for yourself," she said solemnly, and when I did not show interest in this idea she added: "Anyway, it is a sin to be idle."

I liked my family, all of them, but best of all I loved Katie. I loved her not only because she was kind but because she was beautiful, with her hair a cloud about her face, her tiny waist, her pretty dresses. My mother said she resembled her father who had been a cavalry officer. I soon learned that Katie at seventeen was in love with Joe, a tall young man with long thin fingers and the temperament of an opera star.

My new family gradually made my other family in far-away Avialano recede into the past. But now and then, when I felt unhappy and thought my father cold or my mother preoccupied, I would imagine myself back with Taddeo. At such times I would take my red confirmation dress from the box, and the white kerchief Mamarella had tied under my chin, and, putting on my finery, would imagine myself back in Avialano.

In four months I was able to speak English well enough to enjoy the school I attended — Public School Number One. This school still had the characteristics of what it had formerly been, a charity school, one of the last so-called

13

"soup schools." It was in several adjoining old brownstone houses and was in the charge of two old ladies who opened classes each morning with prayer and the singing of "Columbia, the Gem of the Ocean."

When I was ready for the third grade we moved from East Harlem. Mother had at last convinced Father that she could no longer bear to live this cluttered life of the tenements. So we moved to a house in Westchester, but this house did not prove satisfactory either. We moved several times. Finally, Father established a successful grocery business, and several years later Mother took over a large house with tillable acreage near Castle Hill. In this home the rest of my youth was spent.

There were sixty-four acres of land and a big rambling house. Mother had coveted this farm before we went to live on it. It was the property of Mattie and Sadie Munn, two maiden ladies who lived near us. They were old and Mother took care of Miss Sadie, who was an invalid. She also looked after their house, and the old ladies grew to depend on her. It was when they died that we went to live in the house.

The former occupants had called the colonial house "Pilgrim's Rest." There were no lights but kerosene lamps. The roof leaked and there was only an outside toilet. But from the first I loved this home dearly and especially my own room on the second floor which was literally in the arms of a huge horsechestnut tree, lovely at all times but especially so when its flowers, like white candles, were lighted in the spring.

Our home was full of children all the time. My brothers' youngsters came and went. Katie brought her baby over often. In addition, there were dogs, cats, chickens, geese, and now and then a goat or pig. Mother fed everyone well. She bought so much feed for the chickens and for the wild birds who knew ours as a generous temporary home that Father complained that she spent more on feed than she made on eggs. This I doubt, for Mother was a good manager. She ran her farm with hired helpers but she was the best worker of all. We grew all sorts of produce, enough for ourselves and some to sell in Father's store and some was also sent to Washington Market.

We had little cash, but we had a house, a slice of good earth, and a resourceful mother, one with imagination. We were not conscious of want or insecurity even when there was no money. I remember one particular dessert she made for us children when money was scarce. We were always delighted when she mixed new-fallen snow and sugar and coffee, and made for us her version of *granita de caffé*.

We had neighbors all about us — Scotch, Irish, and German families. There were two Catholic churches not far from us, Holy Family Church largely attended by the German population and St. Raymond's attended by the Irish Catholics. We did not seem to belong in either church and Father and Mother soon ceased to receive the Sacraments and then stopped going to church. But Mother still sang songs of the saints and told us religious stories from the storehouse of her memories.

Though we still considered ours a Catholic family we were no longer practicing Catholics. Mother urged us children to go to church but we soon followed our parents' example. I think my mother was self-conscious about her poor English and lack of fine clothes. Though the crucifix was still over our beds and Mother burned vigil lights before the statue of Our Lady, we children got the idea that such things were of the Italian past, and we wanted to be Americans. Willingly, and yet not knowing what we did, we cut ourselves off from the culture of our own people, and set out to find something new.

For me the search began in the public schools and libraries. There was a public school a half-mile from our house — Number Twelve. Dr. Condon, the principal, a man of varying interests, was fond of having his pupils march to the school fife-and-drum corps. He was apt to interrupt classes and call on everyone to go marching, the fife-and-drum players in the lead. In this school there was Bible reading daily by Dr. Condon himself. I learned to love the psalms and proverbs that he read to us and to admire their poetic language.

Near our house on Westchester Avenue was St. Peter's Episcopal Church and on Castle Hill was the rectory. In architecture and landscape, St. Peter's looked like pictures of English churches. Its grounds extended a half-mile or more. In summer we picked blackberries there and in the spring we hunted violets and star of Bethlehem.

St. Peter's was an old church; in its graveyard were headstones with weather-dimmed names. Sometimes on Sunday afternoons I wandered through the graveyard trying to reconstruct the people from their names. Because of my constant reading of books on American history I thought of them all as Pilgrims and Puritans or heroes of the Civil War. I frequently placed bouquets of flowers on these graves as a token of respect to the men and women of an American past. I wanted passionately to be a part of America. Like a plant, I was trying to take roots. We had cut our ties with our own cultural past and it was difficult to find a new cultural present.

The minister at St. Peter's, Dr. Clendenning, was a dignified and kindly gentleman whom we greeted as he walked or rode from the rectory to the church. Across from St. Peter's was a building for church activities which I passed on my way to school. It was near the Huntington Library and I became friendly with the librarian. She was

16

interested in children who liked books and it was she who suggested that I go to the afternoon sewing circle at St. Peter's parish house.

In charge of this work was Gabrielle Clendenning, the minister's daughter. We met once a week and we sewed and sang. It was here that I first learned such simple songs as "Onward, Christian Soldiers" and "Rock of Ages Cleft for Me." The other children used to cross the street and go to services in the church. I drew the line at joining them in this because I regarded myself as a Catholic, though actually I was conscious of almost no tie to my own Church. I explained to Miss Gabrielle that Catholics were not permitted to attend any other church. She seemed to understand and she never objected or argued with me about it.

When the children came back from services, we all had tea and cookies together. It was a most happy association. Often Gabrielle Clendenning invited the children to ride with her in her pony cart. That was high adventure for me; and it meant being accepted among people I loved. Gabrielle's mother, the librarian told me, was the daughter of Horace Greeley. I didn't know who Horace Greeley was but she told me he had been a famous editor and a patriotic American. I remember this family as a wholesome influence on our neighborhood. They set the pattern for what I believed to be the American character.

Life in that little community was peaceful. Our cluster of houses was filled with people who respected each other despite differences of race or religion. We were not conscious of the differences but of the kindnesses to each other. Mr. Weisman the druggist and Mrs. Fox the candy-store owner, the McGraths and the Clendennings and the Visonos — all lived together with not the slightest sense of hostility or of inequality. We accepted our differences and respected each person for his own qualities. It was a good place for a child to grow up.

Several years before I graduated from Public School Number Twelve, World War I had commenced. I became an avid reader of newspapers. I read the gruesome propaganda charging the Germans with atrocities. My imagination was stirred to fever pitch. I never lost the newspaper habit after that. And what I read left its imprint upon me.

In the fall of 1916 I was ready for Evander Childs High School. But I did not enter for another year, a hard and terrible year for me. I was coming home on the trolley car one hot day in July and I had signaled the motorman to let me off. The trolley stopped, and I don't know what happened next, but I was flung into the street and my left foot went under the wheels.

I did not faint. I lay in the street till my father came to me, picked me up in his arms, and with tears streaming down his face, carried me to a physician. I was in great pain by the time an ambulance arrived, but the doctor who sat beside me was so kind that I hated to give him trouble. So we joked together all the way to Fordham Hospital.

As they carried me in, I fainted. When I came back to consciousness there was the sickly smell of ether and pain that stabbed mercilessly. The look on Mother's face as she sat beside my bed told me something was terribly wrong. I learned that same day that my left foot had been amputated.

Mother came faithfully to the hospital, loaded with oranges and flowers and whatever she thought would interest me. It was a hot, sultry summer. There was a strike on the trolley system and Mother had to walk many miles to the hospital. She never missed a single visiting day during that dreadful year.

It was a bitter time for me. I was in the women's ward, for I was tall for my age. I saw women in pain and saw them die. I was particularly affected by one old lady, who came to the hospital with a broken hip and died of gangrene when they amputated her leg. I could not sleep that night, nor many nights thereafter.

My wound did not heal well. I was in that hospital almost a year — treatment after treatment, operation after operation, with little improvement. Five times I was taken to the operating room; five times there was the sickening smell of ether. The day I felt most desolate was the day school opened and I saw from the hospital window children going by with books in their arms. I was so sad that young Dr. John Conboy stopped to ask what was wrong.

"I was going to start high school today," I told him through my tears. "Now I'll be behind the rest in Latin." For Latin was the subject I had looked forward to most of all; it was to me the symbol of a real education.

That afternoon Dr. Conboy brought me the Latin grammar he had used in college and promised to help me. I promptly started to work at it.

During the time I was in the hospital I was registered as a Catholic but I never saw anyone from my Church. Occasionally a priest came through the ward, but I was too shy to call to him. However, Dr. Clendenning and Gabrielle came, and they wrote me letters. Once Dr. Clendenning brought me a little book of religious poems and sayings. On the white cover were flowers, and the frontispiece was a reproduction of "The Gleaners" and the title: *Palette d'Or.* I read and reread this book.

When it was evident that the surgical operations were resulting in nothing but pain, Mother decided to take me home. I spent the next six months on the farm and Mother nursed me. I went about on crutches until an apparatus

19

could be fitted to my foot. A general practitioner came to our house to treat me once a week, for the operation had not been well done and the wounds healed slowly. I spent most of my time reading and writing poetry and developing my friendship with my mother. I was so glad to be away from the hospital that I felt almost content.

During this period our family suffered losses by death. My sister Katie lost her second baby and not long afterward she herself died in the influenza epidemic. Mother suffered terribly and her brown hair became white. It pained me to see her suffer so. Her sons were married and gone from home; one daughter was dead, the other an invalid.

During that time at home I spent most of my time reading. My mother brought me books from the local library, and I read the accumulation left in our house by the Munns. Since that family had been Methodist, the books included a variety of hymnbooks, old Bibles, and commentaries, and the sermons of John Wesley. There was also a copy of a book by Sheldon called *In His Steps* which made a profound impression upon me.

The old Bibles had fascinating illustrations over which I pored. I liked the sermons of John Wesley. Even today his sturdiness comforts me, so firm and straight like the English oaks under which he stood to talk to his congregation.

There was, of course, a great deal of the Gospel simplicity in these old worn books and out of them I distilled a little prayer of my own which never left me. Even when I did not believe any more, I would often repeat the words as one does a favorite poem. This prayer which I worked out of the books of John Wesley was: "Dear God, save my soul and forgive my sins, for Jesus Christ's sake. Amen."

CHAPTER THREE

In the fall of 1917 I started at Evander Childs High School although my condition had improved little and I had to use crutches. Mother encouraged my going, and often she told me of saints who had endured physical deformity. She made me feel I could accomplish anything I set my heart on, despite my physical limitation.

So I began my high-school years armed with crutches and high hopes. I walked the ten blocks to school and took my place with my class. From the beginning I asked no favors, and teachers and classmates soon realized how I felt and respected my independence.

That winter I got my first apparatus for walking. It was not very good, but it was better than the crutches. Now I really began to enter into school activities. I tried to do everything the other students did, even to going on hikes. I joined the Naturalists' Club and went with members to the Palisades, hunting flowers and spotting birds. If I got tired, I sat down for a while till the others returned.

21

During those days, despite my difficulties, I was a happy girl. I loved life dearly and found pleasure in many little things. Sometimes, when outdoors, I would stop to listen, for I felt the whole world whispering to me. The spring wind seemed to talk of things far away and beautiful. Sometimes at night, when the moon shone through the chestnut tree beside my window and I could smell the iris and lilacs and lilies of the valley, I felt tears in my eyes and I did not know why.

The student body at Evander Childs High School then numbered more than a thousand boys and girls. They were mostly the children of Americans of Scottish, Irish, and German extraction but there were also some children of Italian, Russian, and other European peoples. We were of all faiths — Protestant, Catholic, Jewish. We were alike in that we were children of parents in modest circumstances, neither rich nor poor. No one attempted to accentuate our differences or to exploit them.

One day a girl from the East Bronx with whom I had talked about politics, a subject which was beginning to interest me, brought me a copy of a paper I had never seen before. *The Call* was a Socialist publication. That paper gave a new turn to my thinking. I sought other copies. I felt my heart beat with excitement as I read the articles on social justice. Even the poetry on the conditions of the poor, on the inequalities of their lives, held my interest. In fact, for the first time I felt a call, a vocation. Unconsciously I enlisted, even if only emotionally, in the army of those who said they would fight social injustice, and I began to find the language of defiance intoxicating. A stubborn pride developed in my own ability to make judgments.

At high school I could not take the usual physical-education courses so I was allowed a study hour with Miss

22

Genevieve O'Connell, the gym teacher, who gave me courses in anatomy and hygiene. She was the only religious influence I encountered in high school. When she learned I was a Catholic, she invited me to attend with her the meetings of a girls' club at the Cenacle of St. Regis in New York City. On Saturday afternoons she and I met a small group of girls and went to the convent at 140th Street and Riverside Drive.

Once there we sat in a circle and sewed simple garments for the poor while a nun read to us. I was not interested in the books read, but the simplicity, the calm, the acceptance of something real and unchanging, did affect me.

The Cenacle did not give direct answers to the questions I was beginning to ask, perhaps because I did not ask them aloud. But I went to several week-end retreats and I was so attracted by the atmosphere of the house that I asked to come for a private retreat. This proved a failure. I was so untaught in things spiritual and so ignorant of matters of the Faith that I could get no meaning from the spiritual readings given by the nun assigned to guide me.

Despite this failure I know that those week ends at the Cenacle did give me something valuable and lasting. I sensed there the deep peace of the spiritual life and I was moved by the Benediction service which I attended for the first time in my life. The brief prayers, the incense, the monstranced Host uplifted, the music, were a poem of faith to me who loved poetry. Many, many times in my later wanderings, at odd moments there stole back to my mind the *Tantum ergo* sung by the nuns in that lovely little chapel.

But though my heart wanted to accept that which I felt stirring within me I could not, for I already had an encrusted pride in my own intellect which rejected what I felt was unscientific. In this I reflected the superficial patter, prevalent in educational circles of that time, about science being opposed to religion.

During my four years at Evander Childs I received good marks in English history and science, and I won a state scholarship which helped me to go to college. On graduation day I held tight to my diploma and to the copies of Shelley and Keats which were my prizes for excellence in English. Proud as I was of the prizes, my chief pride was that I had been chosen the most popular girl in my class.

In the autumn I entered Hunter, the New York City college for women. I had decided to become a teacher. I started with a determination to learn. There were many fields I wanted to explore. I lived at home and traveled back and forth each day on the new Pelham Bay Subway, recently extended to our neighborhood.

My first college wardrobe consisted of two dresses, a blue voile and a gingham, a black skirt, two sweaters knitted by Mother, and a large collection of starched white collars which I wore with my sweaters. Today the wardrobe of a girl in college, no matter how poor, undoubtedly would be larger, but I was never conscious of an inadequate wardrobe. That was a feature of Hunter College, for the students, even those from well-to-do homes, were more interested in things of the mind.

College proved different from high school and at first seemed duller. The coeducational high school had been more challenging. Hunter College was at that time in a state of transition, passing from a female academy for the training of teachers into a real college. Although accredited to give degrees, the atmosphere and the staff were still the same as when it had been a genteel teacher-training institute.

Because of this difference there was an undefined sense

of distance between faculty and students accentuated by the fact that some of the staff members constantly reminded us that we were getting a free education from the city and should be grateful. There was a current of resentment among the students who felt we were getting only that to which we were entitled.

Dean Annie Hickenbottom was a fine woman, middle-aged, gracious, and well-bred, herself a graduate of Hunter Normal School. We girls loved her, but in a patronizing way. We listened to her politely more with our ears than our minds when she told us, as she often did, how important it was for Hunter girls to wear hats and gloves and to speak only in low and refined voices.

Though the staff was chiefly made up of the old Protestant Anglo-Saxon, Scotch, and Irish Americans, there were a few exceptions. There were several Catholics in the Education Department, and a few Jewish teachers, among them Dr. Adele Bildersee, who taught English and who often talked to her pupils about the beauty of the great Jewish holidays and read aloud to us the ancient prayers and writings in a voice that showed how she loved and admired their beauty and believed in their truth.

The gentle lady who taught medieval history, Dr. Elizabeth Burlingame, was considered overly sentimental by some of the staff. Perhaps she was. Yet I owe her a deep gratitude for the appreciation of the Middle Ages which she gave me. From her came no cold array of facts but a warm understanding of the period. She gave me a love of the thirteenth century and a realization of the role of the Catholic Church in that era. Unfortunately her teaching was of a past we considered dead.

The teacher who affected me most as a person was Sarah Parks, who taught freshman English. Her teaching had little of the past; it was of the present and the future.

She was different from the rest of the well-mannered faculty members. More unorthodox than any of the students dared to be, she came to school without a hat, her straight blond hair flying in the wind as she rode along Park Avenue on her bicycle.

Evidently Dean Annie Hickenbottom said nothing about it to Miss Parks. Nevertheless we students knew well what she would have said had she seen us riding down Sixty-eighth Street on a bicycle and hatless! She would have been scandalized. I am certain she would have been more scandalized by some of Miss Parks's advanced social theories. But in this period at Hunter the classroom was the teacher's castle and no one would dare intrude. Miss Parks's social theories were to me both disturbing and exciting.

During my first year at Hunter I joined the Newman Club, only to lose interest in it very quickly, for aside from its social aspect all its other activities seemed purely formal. There was little serious discussion of the tenets of the Faith and almost no emphasis on Catholic participation in the affairs of the world. In my young arrogance I regarded its atmosphere as anti-intellectual.

The faculty adviser of the Club was a dear little lady who seemed to me to be so far removed from reality that she could not possibly span the wide gap between the cloistered isolation of her own life and the problems facing the students. After awhile I gave up making suggestions for discussion and no longer tried to integrate myself in the Newman Club, even though it still seemed the reasonable place for me to be. I was finding it difficult to determine where I belonged. For the first time I began to feel uneasy.

I drifted into another circle of friends, girls with a strong intellectual drive permeated with a sense of responsibility for social reform. My best friend was Ruth Goldstein. Often I went to her home where her mother, a wise, fine woman with an Old Testament air about her, fed us with her good cooking and gave us sound advice.

On the Jewish holidays of Rosh Hashana and the Passover Mrs. Goldstein invited me to meals and the family services. The age-old ceremonies impressed me; it was inspiring to see how this family remained true to the history of its people, how in this new land they strengthened their sense of oneness with the past by prayer. As I watched the candles glow and heard the Hebrew prayers I was conscious of the fact that my family was not so bound together, and now did not seem to belong anywhere. In spite of our devoted parents, we children seemed to be drifting in different directions.

At Hunter College there were also the children of many foreign-born people. I became friendly with several girls whose parents had been in the Russian Revolution of 1905. They had grown up hearing their parents discuss socialist and Marxist theories. Though they sometimes laughed at their parents they were the nucleus of the communist activities to come, full of their parents' frustrated idealism and their sense of a Messianic mission.

My friends at Hunter College were from all groups. I was received by all but felt part of none. I spent many hours in discussions with different groups. Down in the basement of the Sixty-eighth Street building was a room which we had turned into an informal tearoom and meeting place. There we developed a sort of intellectual proletariat of our own. We discussed revolution, sex, philosophy, religion, unguided by any standard of right and wrong. We talked of a future "unity of forces of the mind," a "new tradition," a "new world" which we were going to help build out of the present selfish one.

27

Since we had no common basis of belief, we drifted into *laissez-faire* thinking, with agnosticism for our religion and pragmatism for our philosophy. There were religious clubs at Hunter at this time. The group I traveled with regarded them as social clubs which you could take or leave, as you chose. A few among us dared say openly, "There is no God." Most of us said, "Maybe there is and maybe there isn't."

There were a few communists on the campus at the time, but they were of little importance. They were a leather-jacketed, down-at-the-heels group, who showed little interest in making themselves understood or in trying to understand others. Their talk was chiefly about the necessity of ending the concentration of wealth in the hands of a few families, and a glorification of the Russian Revolution. They were also interested in good music and European literature and read the "opinion" magazines, such as *The Nation* and *The New Republic*.

My own religious training had been superficial. As a child I had gone to church with Mamarella. I had been taught to say my prayers. In our house hung various holy pictures and the crucifix. But I knew nothing of the doctrines of my faith. I knew much more of the dogmas of English composition. If I held any belief it was that we should dedicate ourselves to love of our fellow man.

Sarah Parks spurred us on to the new and the untried. From her I first heard favorable talk about the Russian Revolution. She compared it with the French Revolution which she said had had a great liberalizing effect on European culture, something which the revolution in Russia would also one day accomplish. It was she who had brought to class books on communism and loaned them to those of us who wanted to read them.

During my first year with her as my teacher I wrote two

term themes, one on how to grow roses, the other on monasticism. She gave both good grades, but the one on monasticism bore the ominous little order, "See me." She was too honest not to give a good grade if the work was well done, but she also had to speak her mind on the subject matter.

When I came in, she seemed sympathetic and asked how I came to choose such a topic. I tried to tell her about my reading in the medieval history course and how impressed I had been with the selfless men and women of the Middle Ages who served mankind by putting self aside.

"And does that seem a normal manifestation of living to you, a seventeen-year-old girl?" she asked scornfully.

It was a question I could not answer, and her clever scorn raised doubts in my mind.

At the end of my freshman year I decided that I must earn money to help with expenses for the next year. So I got a job selling books, a rather daring choice since I still had difficulty in walking any great distance without pain.

The book I sold that summer was called the *Volume Library*, a tome filled with facts and items of information for children. It cost from nine to fifteen dollars, depending on the binding. My sales area was a section of Westchester County. Since it was some distance from home, I rented a room in the home of a farmer's family near Mt. Kisco.

All summer I sold books, and I proved a good agent. It was tiring work but I made enough money that summer to keep myself in clothes and pocket money and for my school expenses the following year.

In the autumn I returned to Hunter. I was a different girl in many ways from the one I was when I entered college the year before. In a year my thinking had changed. I now talked glibly of science and the evolution of man and society and I was skeptical of religious concepts. I had drifted into an acceptance of the idea that those who believed in a Creator were anti-intellectual, and that belief in an afterlife was unscientific. I was tolerant of all religions. They were fine, I said, for those who needed them, but for a human being who was able to think for herself there was no need of something to lean on. One could stand erect alone. This new approach to life was a heady thing. It caught me up and held me.

That second year I did not have Sarah Parks as a teacher. But I often talked with her, for she invited some of us to her apartment, and we sought her advice as if she were a kind of unofficial dean.

To us who loved her Sarah Parks brought fresh air into a sterile, intellectual atmosphere where scholarship sometimes seemed pointless and where Phi Beta Kappa keys were garnered by grinds. We began to speak with contempt about grades and degrees. I remember we held one discussion on whether a true intellectual should accept keys at all, since they were based on marks and used to stimulate the competitive instinct of the rabble and often did not represent true intellectual worth. We held that we must be moved by a desire for real learning and for co-operation with other scholars, and not by a spirit of competition.

Miss Parks led a busy life because so many of us wanted to consult her. She was an important factor in preparing us to accept a materialist philosophy by mercilessly deriding what she called "dry rot" of existing society. I am sure she did help some students, but she did little for those who were already so emptied of convictions that they believed in nothing. These could only turn their steps toward the great delusion of our time, toward the socialist-communist philosophy of Karl Marx.

She questioned existing patterns of moral behavior and diverted some of us into a blind alley by her pragmatic approach to moral problems. In that sex-saturated period of the twenties, the intellectual young were more interested in the life around them than in the promises of the spirit. It was the day of the "flapper," of bobbed hair, of fringed skirts and shapeless dresses, of spiritual blight, and of physical dominance. We considered ourselves the intelligentsia and developed our own code of behavior. Contemptuous of the past and nauseated by the crudeness and ugliness of the period, we regarded ourselves the *avant-garde* of a new culture.

In my junior year I was elected president of my class. Several of my friends and I became involved with student self-government. It was another opportunity to achieve a sense of importance, to express impatience with our elders, and at the same time to feel we were doing something for our fellow students to exhibit that sense of social mission. To Student Council meeting bright young girls brought in all sorts of dazzling proposals and I, ready to support the experimental and the new, listened eagerly to them all. Our little group grew vocally indignant as we read of fortunes amassed by people whose hardest labor was pulling the ticker tape in a Wall Street office. It was a period of ostentatious vulgarity in the city, and our group became almost ascetic to show its scorn of things material.

As I look back on that febrile group, so eager to help the world, looking about for something to spend themselves on, our earnestness appears pathetic. We had, all of us, a strong will to real goodness. We saw a bleak present and wanted to turn it into a wonderful future for the poor and the troubled. But we had no foundation for solid thinking or effective action. We had no real goals because we had no sound view of man's nature and destiny. We had feelings and emotions, but no standards by which to chart the future.

31

Later in my junior year I attended with Mina Rees, the Student Council president, an intercollegiate conference at Vassar College. Vassar made us feel at home during the five days we were there. The days and evenings at the dormitories where we stayed were filled with good talk and an exhilarating exchange of ideas.

Many things were discussed at the conference, among them sororities and their possible abolition. Not belonging to a sorority had never troubled me. Now, listening to sharp criticisms of them by a group of delegates, I felt that I had not been too alert regarding this problem. I had always considered them rather infantile but the conference seemed to consider them a social problem.

We discussed the importance of an honor system under student supervision. In line with discussion of the honor system we talked about the question of the punishment of crime: was it to be considered a penalty or a deterrent? The dominant group thought it should be considered only as the latter. But I spoke up and said that surely it should be considered both.

In my senior year I was elected president of Student Council. That year I led the movement to establish the honor system at Hunter. Also in that year I brought politics into student self-government by conducting the first straw vote in the presidential elections. A little later I upset Dean Hickenbottom by insisting on a series of lectures on social hygiene. I was supported by a group of school politicians and I learned the value of a tightly organized group and was exhilarated by the power it gave.

During the previous year Professor Hannah Egan, who taught in the Education Department, stopped me one day in the hall. "Why don't you ever come to the Newman Club?" she asked.

32

I tried to find a polite excuse as well as a valid one. Noting my confusion, she said sternly, "Bella Visono, ever since you were elected to Student Council and became popular you have been heading straight for hell."

I was flabbergasted. This, I thought, seemed very old-fashioned. But I was dismayed too. I consoled myself by repeating a line from *Abu Ben Adhem*: "Then write me as one who loves his fellow men." That idea cheered me considerably. I threw off the personal responsibility Miss Egan was trying to load on me. The important thing, I said, was to love my fellow man.

This was the new creed, the creed of fellowship, and it was clear the world needed it badly. It was a fine phrase which kept some of the significance of the Cross even while it denied the divinity of the Crucified. It was a creed that willingly accepted pain and self-immolation; but it was skeptical of a promised redemption. I kept reassuring myself that I did not need the old-fashioned Creed any more. I was modern. I was a follower of science. I was going to spend my life serving my fellow men.

In June 1925 I was graduated with honors. Commencement had brought the necessity of thinking about my immediate future. I had already taken the examinations for teaching in both elementary and high schools in New York City and because of the scarcity of teachers I was certain of a position.

The day after commencement I was at Ruth Goldstein's home. We had both enrolled for the summer session at Columbia University, intent on getting masters' degrees, and her older sister Gertrude startled us both by asking why we were going to Columbia at all. "Now that college is over, you girls must get a job — and also a man," she said.

Ruth and I smiled at her words. They did, however, start

a chain of thought. During my years at college I had been a student, a politician, a reformer. Now, with time to think, I realized that I was also a woman. I realized also that my education had done little to train me as a woman.

For some time I had known that I must have further surgery on my foot. Now that I was free from school work I made a sudden decision. I went to St. Francis Hospital in the Bronx. Why I chose that hospital I do not know. To the nun who appeared to interview me I said I needed surgery on my foot and I wanted the name of the best surgeon connected with the hospital. She gave me the name of Dr. Edgerton and his office address on Park Avenue. I went immediately to see him.

Dr. Edgerton was a man well over six feet tall and he looked so big and capable that I had confidence in him immediately. I showed him my foot and asked, "What do you think of it?"

His answer was direct and emphatic. "It's a rotten amputation," he said.

"Can you do anything for me?" I asked timidly.

"Of course I can," he said. "A clean-cut amputation and you'll be able to walk easily. I promise you that you will be able to dance and skate six weeks after you leave the hospital."

There was a further important matter to discuss. "How much will it cost?" I asked. He named what was no doubt a modest sum for his services. With a self-confidence that surprised even myself I said, "I have no money at all now, Dr. Edgerton. I'm just out of college but I'll get a job as soon as I am well and then I'll pay you as fast as I can."

He smiled at me. "I'll take a chance," he said, and made arrangements for me to enter St. Francis Hospital the next morning.

I was in excellent hands. The Franciscan nurses in

charge were competent and so were the lay nurse assistants. When I entered the hospital and was questioned as to my religion I said I had been a Catholic but was now a freethinker, making the statement no doubt with youthful bravado.

As I look back on that time I think it was a pity that no one paid attention to my statement regarding religion. The nuns went in and out of my room and were efficient and friendly. Once or twice I saw a priest go by, but none came in to talk to me. No one spoke to me of religious matters while I was there. Had they done so, I might have responded.

Six weeks after I went home I was walking well, as Dr. Edgerton had promised. I soon obtained a position as a substitute teacher in the History Department of Seward Park High School which, with discipline at a low ebb, was considered a hard school. I was to have six classes in medieval and European history.

When I appeared on the scene the students had been without a teacher for weeks and were at the chalk-and-eraser-throwing stage. I came to my teaching with a sense of reverence for the task and a determination to keep to my ideals, but like all young teachers I had to learn that there is a wide gap between theory and practice. It is in the classroom that a teacher learns how to teach. All courses given on methods of teaching are but guideposts to a basic objective.

The boys had evidently decided to test me. On my second day of teaching I came in to find a fire at the back of the room. I walked over to the smoking debris, put out the fire, and collared the four nearest boys.

"Who lit the fire?" I demanded. They denied having anything to do with it. There was nothing more to do at the moment. The fire was out, so the lesson in European his-

35

tory continued. I decided to solve my problem without calling either the head of the department or the assistant principal. I asked one of the older boys for help.

"Evans," I said, "you are older than the rest. Help me with this problem."

Evans scratched his head and said thoughtfully, "Listen, Miss Visono, what you have to do is show them that you can take their gaff. After that they'll settle down."

It was good advice. I worked hard to stimulate interest and they did settle down. The rest of the term passed without any more violent demonstrations.

I tried, in line with my acute interest in politics, to interest my young students. I made them bring newspapers to class and I started lively discussions. Most of the boys brought the tabloids and when I spoke of this choice with some annoyance, one of my students, young Morris Levine, said to me, "Aw, Miss Visono, what do you want me to read — the *Times?* I don't own any stocks and bonds."

The school term at Seward Park was to end at the beginning of February. Sometime after the turn of the new year in 1926, Dr. Dawson, the chairman of the Political Science Department at Hunter College, called and offered me a post at the college. I began teaching at Hunter College in February 1926.

CHAPTER FOUR

THAT SPRING of 1926 I had a full teaching program of fifteen hours a week in freshman political science. Classes were large, and we were crowded for space.

Dr. Dawson, chairman of the department, a Virginian, had been my teacher in all my classes in political science. I knew his temper and his methods. He was a well-mannered gentleman whose method of teaching was unusual, for he simply directed his students to the library and told them to read. In class he never got excited or expressed any passionate opinions. He had taught at Princeton when Woodrow Wilson was president there. He was a Wilsonian Democrat and uncritically supported Wilson and the League of Nations and he believed that the International Court at The Hague was the beginning of international stability. He was a persuasive propagandizer for such reforms as a city manager system, direct primaries, and executive budgets. I had found it easy to accept his beliefs and to make them my own. Never once did we reach fundamental questions on government; all our talk was of superficial formalities.

I had been one of his favorite students because, while many students did little work when given freedom of working, I had thrown myself heart and soul into endless hours of reading in the library, especially the works of De Tocqueville, Lord Bryce, and Charles A. Beard, which gave me an interest in American government and an appreciation of the fundamentals of the Constitution. Because Dr. Dawson was a Virginian, perhaps, we got more than we would otherwise on the subject of states' rights.

I was a teacher myself now, but I had no clear perspective as to the objectives of teaching. I did not know what I expected from my students. In lieu of this I tried to stimulate them, to make them think and argue about public questions, and I hoped to have them ready to take action on these in later life. I wanted to have them learn through practical experience as well as through the textbook.

Ruth Goldstein, Margaret Gustaferro, and I became assistants to Dr. Dawson. In 1926 the avalanche of freshmen found the college unprepared. Facilities were inadequate. We three taught our classes at the same time in different sections of the auditorium which had been used as a chapel. We three young teachers had been close friends at college. Now we worked together, developing curricula, bibliographies, and new techniques. All of us enrolled in the graduate school at Columbia University for graduate work in political science.

At that time many professors were slanting their teaching in the direction known as muckraking. Some professors contended publicly that the war had not been fought to make the world safe for democracy and that Germany had been shamefully treated by the Versailles Treaty. It was also a time when Columbia professors fresh from the London School of Economics and from the Brookings Institute were discovering the importance of current activity in political parties and practical politics. Some were beginning to enlist in local political battles. These sent students through the city, climbing stairs and ringing doorbells, to teach them the democratic process by actual research.

We entered on this new kind of laboratory work with zest. We dissected and analyzed local political bosses with the cynicism of old hands, and then we began to push on into political clubhouses to learn still more of this fascinating profession.

One of my courses at Columbia that year was a study of the United States Senate and its treaty-making powers. Some of the professors wondered audibly why Lindsey Rogers, who taught it, regarded this topic important enough to devote an entire course to it. It was then only six years after the *Missouri v. Holland* decision based on a treaty relating to migratory birds — and the pattern of treaty law had not yet become apparent to many. I was fascinated by the subject and its implications.

There were other refreshingly new courses that year and new professors, among them Raymond Moley, not yet a Roosevelt brain truster. There were courses on the press and on public opinion. We young people were intrigued by the possibilities of participation in government control and the various means of achieving this.

In our enthusiasm we passed on to our students at Hunter what we had learned. We challenged the traditional thinking they had brought to college with them. We sent out girls to political clubs, too. Soon political leaders began to call Hunter to find out what the idea was of sending the "kids" to their clubs.

We did not stop it, however. We sent them in pairs to

visit courts and jails, legislatures and institutions. When a socialist student asked if groups could visit the socialist clubs, too, we accepted the suggestion. We encouraged them to mix with all groups. Before long we were saying — and not yet realizing it was merely a rather meaningless cliché — that the radicals of today are the conservatives of tomorrow, that there could be no progress if there were no radicals.

In the days that have gone since we enunciated these statements so confidently I have had many occasions to see that this cataloging of people as either "right" or "left" has led to more confusion in American life than perhaps any other false concept. It sounds so simple and so right. By using this schematic device one puts the communists on the left and then one regards them as advanced liberals — after which it is easy to regard them as the enzyme necessary for progress.

Communists usurp the position of the left, but when one examines them in the light of what they really stand for, one sees them as the rankest kind of reactionaries and communism as the most reactionary backward leap in the long history of social movements. It is one which seeks to obliterate in one revolutionary wave two thousand years of man's progress.

During my thirteen years of teaching at Hunter I was to repeat this semantic falsehood many times. I did not see the truth that people are not born "right" or "left" nor can they become "right" or "left" unless educated on the basis of a philosophy which is as carefully organized and as all-inclusive as communism.

I was among the first of a new kind of teacher who was to come in great numbers to the city colleges. The mark of the decade was on us. We were sophisticated, intellectually snobbish, but usually fetishly "democratic"

40

with the students. It is true that we understood them better than did many of the older teachers; our sympathy with them was a part of ourselves.

During the afternoons and evenings I continued my work at Columbia. I had Carlton J. H. Hayes on "The Rise of Nationalism." I studied closely A. A. Berle and Gardiner Means who wrote of the two hundred corporations that controlled America at the end of World War I. I read widely on imperialism and began to be critical of the role my country was playing. I discovered the John Dewey Society and the Progressive Education Association. I became aware of the popular concept of the social frontier. I also repeated glibly that we had reached the last of our natural frontiers and that the new ones to be sought must be social. There would be, we were told, in the near future a collective society in our world and especially in our country, and in teaching students one must prepare them for that day.

As a result of that year's study of American history and national politics, as well as in the direct experience of my students and myself in local politics, I now began to tear apart before my students many respected public groups — charity, church, and other organizations — that were trying to better conditions in old-fashioned ways. This sort of talk had a destructive effect on myself, I now realize, and it had an even worse effect on my more sensitive students. If they followed where I led, there was nothing left for them to believe in. I had tried to wreck their former ways of thought and I had given them no new paths to follow. The reason was simple: I had none myself, because I really didn't know where I was going.

Later when, in the Communist Party, I met one of these former students of mine, it was always with the feeling that I was responsible for her present way of life; it was through me that they had accepted this cold, hard faith they lived by.

But in 1926 I had little thought of the communists except that I did not preclude theirs as a solution of problems. I was merely goading my pupils and myself on to feel that we must do something to help set aright the things wrong in the world. When I became emotional in my talks it was because I was angered at those who had money without working for it and who did not help to lessen the increasing misery of the working population.

There were lighter moments in my days, of course. We met for parties and good talk and sometimes went to the bistros of that era of prohibition. Once I took one of the elderly professors at Hunter to a speakeasy, partly as a lark and partly as a kindness, thinking to show her life.

But Bessie Dean Cooper took the evening in her stride. She was a hardy old lady who taught history and gave the whole department color. Her eleven cats were a legend. That evening she asked me if she could leave one of them with me while she went to Europe; friends were taking over the rest. I promised, and turned the cat over to my mother, along with the food and medicines and careful directions and the cat's blanket and pillow. Mother took a look at all this paraphernalia and said briefly, "I feed cats like cats," and did so until their mistress returned. Some years later Miss Cooper retired from Hunter and took the eleven cats to live on the French Riviera.

Frequently during this period I went to Teachers College at Columbia. I was always impressed by the large enrollment of teachers from nearly every state in the union. I watched them as they gathered round the trees which bore the shields of their states. I, too, realized what a powerful effect Teachers College could have on American education with thousands of teachers to influence national policy and social thinking.

That year I learned that George Counts, an associate of John Dewey, like him a philosopher and theorist on education, had gone to Russia. He had, of course, been there before. In fact, he had set up the educational system of the revolutionary period for the Russian Government. He had translated the Russian Primer into English and was eager to have the American teachers study it carefully. He promised a report on Russian schools when he returned.

At this period I was influenced by many institutions around the campus at Columbia as much as by the classes I attended. I became a frequent visitor at International House, to which I was first invited by an economics student from the Philippines. There I met among a great many other people Albert Bachman of the French Department who had taught at Tagore's school in India and who introduced me to handsome students from the Punjab, like myself young and agog over ideas. We met on a level of equality and tolerance and with the hope that a world could be created by the young men and women of all nations in which all people could live and work on free and equal terms. We were not aware of the tight web of power which set the stage for molding our opinions.

That summer gave me my first opportunity to talk to people of other countries and to learn that they, too, were filled with a passionate desire to better their own countries and the world. I began, under the impetus of such talk, to feel in me a desire to be a citizen of the world. It was a desire that made it easy and natural for me to accept communism and its emphasis on internationalism.

As for the past, when I felt a twinge of regret for what I was putting behind me, I ignored it. I accepted the present, with all its undirected selfishness, but I could not really adjust myself to it. More and more I wanted to talk and act only in terms of the future, of a future that would have none of the corruption of the present. It depressed me that people close to me could accommodate themselves to such a present. Only people I did not know, the great mass of unknown human beings, began to awaken in me a poignant sense of kinship. In fact, I began to transfer my personal feelings to this wholly unknown defeated mass. And so it came about that I began to seek my spiritual home among the dispossessed of the earth.

A teacher cannot help but transmit to her students something of what she is and what she believes and I know I did much damage. But the saving grace in my destructive teaching of that time was that in my personal relationships with these students I retained within me something of the essence of what God had meant me to be — a woman, a mother. I loved my students, all of them, the dull, the weak, the strong, the conniving, the twisted. I loved them because they were young and alive, because they were in the process of becoming and had not yet been frozen into a mold by a cynical society or by a conniving power.

I have always enjoyed teaching, for there is in teaching a continual renewing, and in that renewal there is always the promise of that freshness which brings us nearer to perfection. To me freshmen were always a delight as students. They came to college with high resolve, many of them caught by a sense of dedication to learning, and they were not yet pressured by practical considerations of jobs and careers, not yet having to accommodate themselves to the *status quo*. They were like acolytes just learning the ritual. If I had been able, during these years, I would have prayed hard for the retention of this flame in my students. For the flame is there always. It is in them all, but whether later it bursts into a fire that destroys, or flickers to nothing, depends in great measure on the teacher and the goals and standards she sets.

During my first two teaching years I spent endless free hours in the Columbia Library and in Room 300 at the New York Public Library. For my dissertation for the master's degree I chose the subject: "Is Congress a Mirror of the Nation?" My paper came to no conclusions. In fact, when I read it over in typed form, I had the unhappy feeling that Congress was somewhat like those Coney Island mirrors which now exaggerate, now underplay, the real.

During my work on this paper I read hundreds of the brief biographies in the *Congressional Directory,* from the foundation of the Republic to the present, and I found one pattern repeated many times: that of the men who rose from humble beginnings and who struggled to acquire an education. I was impressed by the number who were at first schoolteachers, then put themselves through law school, and later entered politics.

I myself was growing impatient with abstract scholarship, for it seemed to lead nowhere. I hated the emphasis placed in the school system on getting degrees. An M.A. was necessary to hold certain jobs and a Ph.D. was essential for a promotion and an increase in salary. I questioned the value of the many dissertations filed away in the archives. The topics chosen for dissertations seemed more and more inconsequential. And my eager youth longed for significance, for meaning, for participation.

I did not realize what I now know, and have come to know through much turmoil of spirit, that significance is all about us and that it comes from order. There was no order in my life. I had no pattern by which to arrange it. I was moved by feelings and emotions and an accumulation of knowledge which brought me no joy of living.

After I had delivered my dissertations and received my

Master of Arts degree in the summer of 1927, Ruth Goldstein and I, both tired out from the year's hard work,
decided to take a cottage for the summer and get away
from New York. So, with Beatrice Feldman, also a Hunter
College freshman, we rented a cottage on Schroon Lake,
in the Adirondacks.

I was happy to be back in the country. I had not realized
how much I missed the land until I found myself back on
it. A few years before our own home had gone, taken by
the march of progress. During my years at college and of
teaching the community around Pilgrim's Rest had altered
greatly. In place of the straggling countryside of my childhood there was now a bustling community, with apartment houses and subways. We had had to give up our old
house because it was dilapidated and not worth repairing.
The property was sold, the house pulled down, and the
land divided into building lots.

At Schroon Lake, Ruth and Beatrice and I were alone
for days at a time. Our friends came for week ends, however, and then our cottage was filled. We had books but
we did not read much. We spent hours on the lake, and
at times Ruth and Beatrice played tennis and golf while
I sat on the grass and watched. And we talked often until
late into the night, discussing many subjects. We discussed
the theories of John Dewey and of Justice Holmes, we
talked of the philosophy of education, and of practical
questions about life and love and marriage. We debated
the value of many of the things our parents had accepted
without fuss or examination.

There is something idyllic about a group of young
people who seek nothing from each other except companionship. To me, who had seen my own family disintegrate,
this was like a new kind of family. Of course I was not
the only one the members of whose family had gone in

different directions, or the only one who was attaching herself instead to the social family of the like-minded.

It was a period when houses as homes were disappearing in our larger cities, when one-room apartments were becoming popular. Before that, no matter how poor the family, it never had less than three or more rooms. Now the kitchen was pushed into a tiny alcove, the bed was tucked into a closet, and you lived in one modern room, sometimes elegant and large, but still one room. Marriage for the intellectual proletariat became the process of living with a man or a woman in quarters so small that release and satisfaction had to be found outside the home, lest the walls of one room suffocate the dwellers.

One of the pleasantest events of that summer in the Adirondacks was meeting the Finkelsteins, Louis and Carmel, and their children, a lovely little girl, Hadassah, and a baby named Ezra. Carmel came from a distinguished English family and she spoke with a fascinating accent. I thought that in appearance she and her daughter looked like characters out of the Bible. Dr. Louis was a rabbi from the Bronx and he had the face of an apostle. Often his brothers "Hinky" and Maurice would come to visit and I loved to listen to them talking together, each topping the other in gay persiflage. I found them exciting because they were not only well read, not only deeply interested in the arts and in philosophy, but also practical men of affairs who understood politics.

My friendship with the Finkelsteins was to continue for years. In them again I saw the warmth of a family which was like-minded, closely knit, and determined to stay together, impervious to the corroding influences of a large industrial city. I asked myself why it was that other families I knew did not have this ability to hold together. I felt that family stability was in great part due to the cherishing of traditions, to the continuous renewing of the memories of the past which included their friendship with God and a boundless loyalty to each other.

One evening that summer I stayed at home with the children. After some time I saw that Hadassah, who had been trying to go to sleep, had begun to cry for no apparent reason. She was a detached sort of child and I thought she did not like me, but now she let me hold her hand as I talked quietly to comfort her. It was obvious she did not know why she was crying, but when she looked up at me the dark eyes full of tears seemed older than those of a little girl and there was an odd fear in the way she sat close to me and wept. When she finally fell asleep, still holding my hand, I sat there with a strange feeling in me, as if she had been crying over a long past, as if two thousand years had been only one night.

That fall I made a sharp switch in my career. Tired of the sterility of graduate work, Ruth Goldstein and I entered New York University Law School. I taught morning and also evening classes at Hunter College and attended my law classes in the afternoons.

The classes at law school were large, sometimes several hundred students. The case system, which was in almost universal use then, did not hold my interest; I found the method dreary. Despite this I liked the study of the law; it was a discipline worth mastering

I also found the students interesting. In one class I sat next to a young man named Samuel Di Falco who is now a Supreme Court judge. He used to find fault with me for scribbling poetry in my notebook when I should have been working on cases.

Ruth also found fault with my preoccupation with other things than the law. For it was true that while the substance of the law intrigued me, because it was a reflection of the past of society which helped me to understand the present, I was not interested in legal procedure, which I felt was intended to preserve an outmoded *status quo*. My constant preoccupation with the need to change the *status quo* made me almost impatient with much of the last year of law school. But I did not expect to practice law. I thought of myself as a teacher.

CHAPTER FIVE

FROM THE FALL of 1927 to June 1930 I attended New York University Law School and taught at Hunter College. It was a period in which I was deeply involved in the activities of the students in my own college — a period in which I was not only instructor but served as adviser to many of them, individually and in their group activities.

As a young instructor disturbed by the conflicting currents among the intellectuals I turned to Sarah Parks for advice and clarification. But the teacher I had admired when I was an undergraduate was embroiled in controversy over salary and promotion policies in the college. These were subjects in which I was not interested at that time, for I loved my position as teacher so much that the salary question seemed secondary. But Sarah was aflame over inequities of rank and salary, and for her sake I tried to interest myself in these matters.

This was a period in which I was meeting men and

women who were talking ideas and living unorthodox lives. It was a period in which a love of literature, the arts, and an interest in the Russian Revolution became the excuse for leaving home and living in little, cramped apartments in Greenwich Village. It was a period in which we spent long hours, night after night, sitting before fireplaces in some Village garret, talking endlessly.

Sarah had been one of us, but now her absorption with college politics had a quality of desperation. I did not feel that the situation warranted the extremes of emotion she poured into it. I did not know then that I, too, was to follow in her footsteps. At this time I sensed only that a certain emptiness in her life was catapulting her violently into everything she did. I tended to withdraw from our close friendship and to cultivate new friends who built on the foundation she had helped to establish.

When in January 1928 she committed suicide I was thrown into an emotional tailspin. I felt guilty at not having spent more time with her. I thought I had failed her. I was bitter about those at the college to whom she had turned for affection and who, instead, had shut the door upon her. Her death had a profound effect on those of us whom she had influenced. We felt that Sarah had the intellectual courage to believe in the new coming collective society, but not the practical boldness required for becoming a disciplined member of the group. We felt that she thought as a collectivist but fought and lived as an individualist and in our twisted estimate of a human life we felt that this was her failure. We did not recognize that life had become unbearable to her because of the disorder of her thinking which inevitably led to self-destruction.

Careful not to continue on the path which led to her suicide I was to take a longer, more deceptive yet parallel road to annihilation. I refused to retrace my steps to the point of departure into wrong thinking. I did not know then that this could bring only disharmony, confusion, and defeat.

The years 1928 and 1929 were replete with confusion and ugliness. I turned more and more to the literature of despair. I tried to write, but found that my inner confusion reflected itself in my work. For the first time in my life I viewed the future with apprehension. I found little pleasure in anything. My work at law school was mediocre. At Hunter College the classes were getting larger and the students coming to us from the high schools were not well prepared. The sense of dedication to learning was receding.

Many came to college because they were fulfilling for their parents the modern yearning of the uneducated who are determined that their children must have a college education. I was conscious of an increasing mass of young people entering college almost as automatically as they entered grade school and high school. I was aware of the lowering of standards. There was little thinking about the meaning and purpose of a college education and practically no thought of the role of free municipal colleges.

During the spring of 1930 I took the Medina cram courses and prepared for the examination for admission to the New York Bar. The examination over, I requested a leave of absence from the college and with my friend Beatrice left for Europe. In a foolish kind of way I hoped to find there answers which were not forthcoming at home. I was tired and restless. I wanted to escape from all sense of responsibility. I was young and I wanted to enjoy life.

It was a trip rich in new contacts. With a capacity to make friends I found people of interest in every walk of life in the different countries we visited. It was on this trip that I was to meet my future husband, John Dodd.

52

We landed in Hamburg and I found it an exciting city, filled with merchant seamen, longshoremen, soldiers. There were the *nouveau riche* with pockets bulging with the country's wealth. There were Communists everywhere, marching, singing, meeting. There were the decadent risqué night spots. There were also fine old restaurants, old homes and churches, and other evidences of an earlier day. It was a city of contrasts.

Too frequently we came face to face with middle-class Germans with pinched, strained faces, ready, when they noted sympathy, to tell you their troubles. The thing that struck me was their bewilderment. They neither understood the cause of their predicament nor where they were going. We looked at them and listened. But we were Americans with dollars in our purses bent on having a good time.

In Berlin we saw more pinched faces and more blatant lavishness. We were alarmed at the frank and open evidences of sexual and moral degradation flaunted in the night spots and exhibited to the tourists everywhere. The atmosphere of the city seemed charged as the air is before an electric storm.

I found some of my friends from Hunter College at the University of Berlin and we had the opportunity to see what was happening at the seats of learning. We talked with university students and professors. The university was torn with strife. Socialists, Communists, National Socialists were battling each other and jointly undermining those who regarded themselves as conservatives attached to their own country by the natural love of one's homeland. Acts of violence were common in the city and around the university.

I was conscious of the fact that here politics had become a matter of life and death. I was conscious also that the intellectuals, the teachers, professors, and scientists were

53

arrogant in their pride but lacked the inner strength to play a salutary role in that country's hour of need. Here were men of the highest intellectual achievements who were ready to attach themselves to the forces of violence. I did not then realize, as I now do, that for close to a century the educational world of Germany had been subjected to systematic despiritualization which could result only in the dehumanization now apparent. This made it possible for such despiritualized men to serve both the Nazi and later the communist power with a terrifying loyalty and efficiency.

In Germany I frequently discussed the rising tide of conflict, but on one thing professors and students alike were agreed — that fascism could never come to Germany. It was possible in Italy, they said, because of the lack of general education — such a thing could not happen in Germany. Two institutions would prevent this: the great German universities and the German Civil Service.

When, contrary to their statements, it did happen in Germany, the two great institutions which collapsed first of all were — the German universities and the German Civil Service. They were the first to serve the Fuehrer, and it was from them that we were to learn the lesson that education in and of itself is not a deterrent to the destruction of a nation. The real questions to be posed are: what kind of education? to what purpose? with what goal? under what standards?

I was happy to leave Berlin. And now I insisted on a trip which was not on our schedule. I had hitherto generally refused to spend much time in museums and churches but I wanted to go to Dresden and see the Sistine Madonna. It was worth the long trip to see the lovely Virgin and Child and the cherubs at their feet looking like gay little urchins. The day I spent in Dresden was my happiest in Germany.

54

I was looking forward to Vienna. It was fortunate that Beatrice had relatives in that fabulous capital of the Hapsburgs. But once again we were struck by the pain in the pinched white faces of the native Austrians. We wore our simplest clothes in order not to give offense to the people we met. We had wanted to go to the opera. In an act of renunciation we decided against it because we had watched men and women who loved music stand outside the opera house while tourists and profiteers jammed the place.

Beatrice's uncle, who had been a financial adviser in the regime of Franz Joseph, entertained us by taking us to some famous coffeehouses. As he talked of the history of Vienna, I became aware of the fact that he loved the city deeply but recognized it was dying. He told us he had made arrangements to take his family to Uruguay. Once again I was struck by the fact that those who deplored the blight that was upon them had no standard to which to rally. They were frightened. There was a sense of *Weltschmerz* and a longing to return to the past, but not the slightest awareness as to where they were going.

From Austria we went to Italy. I had looked forward with ill-concealed excitement to a return to the land of my birth. I expected the sense of not belonging which was part of me suddenly to disappear. I was counting on a mystical transformation. We crossed the border, the customs inspector delved through our luggage, we arrived in Venice, and went to a hotel with a German name. But I searched in vain to find the Italy which my memory had treasured and my imagination had embellished.

Venice was a highly sophisticated, gay, brittle, materialistic city. It was overrun by men in uniform. Practically one out of three was a soldier. I went to the Cathedral, but was unmoved by the services. It was crowded with well-

55

dressed people of all nations. Outside, the merchants drove sharp bargains with those who had money. The spiritual, brooding quality of Italy which I had treasured was nowhere apparent and I realized that I did not belong in the country I had left as a child. I now saw the tangible evidence of the blight of fascist philosophy.

As a student at Hunter College in the early twenties I had declared myself an anti-fascist at a time when it was not fashionable to do so. It had been an emotional declaration against those smug members of society who talked about the wonders that fascism had accomplished for Italy. I felt they were more concerned with train schedules and sanitation than with the beauty of its culture and the soul of its people.

Yet when we reached Florence I found that even fascism was unable to corrode the unbelievably beautiful symbols of the past. I loved being in Florence. The delicate restraint of its scenery and of its architecture seemed to reflect the character of the people themselves. I found myself standing in the public squares and watching the faces of those who went by, struck by the fact that the simplest shopgirl looked like one of Raphael's models.

I was continually amazed to see the diversity and the beauty of the past culture of the cities of Italy. Venice was unlike Florence. Verona and Bologna were a world apart from Rome. In this day, when there is so much talk about mass culture and so many worship, or are frightened into, an acceptance of the idea of one-world government, I look back to the joy I had in the past culture of these little city-states and wonder if the art and architecture of our day will ever achieve the beauty of that of those earlier times.

When I reached Rome I was more interested in the ruins of classical times than in the monuments to the living spirit at the heart of Christianity. It was evidence of how far I, through my education and my own perverse pride of mind, had traveled from the past of my own people and from the accumulated wisdom and safety which two thousand years of Christianity could provide for the modern children of the Western world.

I drove miles in the hot sun to visit the grave of the poet Horace and spent hours at the Baths of Caracalla and other ruins of antiquity, and on a moonlit night I looked with awe on the tiers of the Colosseum and had a sense of the length of its past. I visited the Vatican and some of the churches, but the truth is that I visited them largely for their priceless art treasures and was blind to their real significance.

In Rome the power of the fascist state was everywhere in evidence, especially in the number of men in uniform. I thought suddenly of my mother who had a farmer's disdain of the military. "They all live on our backs," she used to say. And now I thought of Italy as one aching back carrying the vast array of government officials and soldiers.

I had decided to visit the town where I was born to see my foster parents, with whom we had lost touch over the years. However, when I reached Naples there was news of an earthquake so I returned, instead, to Florence. From there we went back into southern Germany for a brief visit.

Beatrice and I went together to Paris, where I picked up my mail at the American Express office. Ruth had cabled, "You passed both parts of the bar exam." My mother and father wrote, "Come home. We are lonely without you."

On the boat returning home I met a group of New York City schoolteachers, who told me they belonged to the Teachers Union. They discussed the importance of having teachers organize within the labor movement and they urged my friend and me to join the Union. When I pointed out that their union consisted largely of public school-teachers and that I did not think that college teachers had any place therein, the persistent recruiters assured me that the brains and the original organizers of the American Federation of Teachers were college teachers. I promised to join as an evidence of my willingness to throw in my lot with the working class, even though I did not think the Union could be of help to me personally.

On my return to New York I went to meetings of the Teachers Union. I found them disconcerting because there was so much strife between groups seeking control. I did not then understand why intelligent adults should struggle so hard to control an organization which in numbers was small and insignificant. I was dumfounded to find the names of distinguished professors such as John Dewey and George Counts involved in the controversy.

It was only later, when I better understood left-wing politics, that I became aware of the significance of control of this beachhead.

CHAPTER SIX

The collapse of the stock market did not immediately affect my family for we had no money invested in stocks or bonds. Therefore it was not difficult for me to leave my post at Hunter College in 1930 to serve a clerkship for admission to the New York Bar. I worked at a nominal salary in the office of Howard Hilton Spellman, who was an excellent lawyer and at that time was writing several texts on corporation law.

During that year I saw a great deal of John Dodd whom I had met on my trip to Europe. At first it seemed we had little in common, for John had an engineer's mind and I was disinterested in all machinery, regarding mechanical devices as a kind of black magic. But we soon discovered topics of common interest, such as our love for this country and an awareness of its problems.

John's family lived in Floyd County, Georgia. Long before I visited his home I had heard him tell the story of how his people had gone into Indian territory and established themselves on the land sixty miles from Atlanta and in the direct line of Sherman's march. He had told me of his grandfather who had lost an arm at the Battle of Shiloh and of his grandmother who had outwitted Sherman's men when they came to her farm; of how his father had turned his land into peach orchards and how he was ruined by railroad rate discrimination that forced Georgia peaches to rot at the siding while California fruit was favored.

When John asked me to marry him, I hesitated. I had given little thought to marriage. I was thinking about a career and those were still the days when women debated marriage or a career, and not marriage and a career. But already economic pressures had pushed many women into business and so limited their activities as homemakers. The women I knew were talking less of homes than they were of dissertations and research. However, I put my doubts aside and we decided to get married.

We did not plan to be married in a church, since John was bitterly anti-clerical. I did not mind the civil marriage; like John, I thought of myself as a freethinker.

One morning in late September we were married at the county clerk's office in New York City. John stood tall and straight and blond, and I beside him, small and dark. Our witnesses were two of my friends — Beatrice Feldman and Dr. Louis Finkelstein.

When the clerk pronounced us man and wife, I had a sudden sinking feeling in my heart. Why? Had I rushed into marriage before I was ready? Was it that this ceremony was not what I had been taught made a marriage? I do not know. I do know that during the next months I grew to love John more than I had thought I was capable of loving anyone.

I knew how devoted he was to the South and its people

60

and after our marriage we went to visit his home. I had never been South before, but I now realized why so many of its children went to Northern cities for a livelihood.

John's people were not plantation owners nor did they have share croppers. They owned a lot of land and they worked it themselves. The women worked as hard as the men. I visited some of the Dodd children at the Martha Berry Schools near John's home and I was struck by the independence and sturdiness of these people. Never after that first visit did I read morbid literature on the South without a sense of resentment at the twisted picture it gave of a section which has great reservoirs of strength, based not on material wealth but upon the integrity of its people.

John was ten years older than I. He had had a variety of experience, having worked in industrial centers, such as Akron and Detroit, and he had seen service as a flier first in the Canadian RAF and later in the American Air Force. In those days of World War I service in that branch was tantamount to joining a suicide squad. As a young soldier he saw many of his comrades killed. He, himself, was in a plane crash at Kelly Field and suffered a spinal injury which left him a highly nervous person.

By 1932 my family felt the results of the depression. My father's business had come to a standstill. John, too, was meeting financial difficulties. I, therefore, decided to return to my post at Hunter College.

I was stunned by the fury of the impact of the depression on my family and those around me. I watched the line of pale, pinched faces of people who stood before the closed doors of the Bowery Savings Bank on Forty-Second Street. They reminded me of the anxious faces I had seen in Hamburg and Berlin a few years before. I saw men obviously once in good circumstances line up around the block for soup and coffee at mission houses. I saw them furtively pick up cigarette butts from the streets.

I had not been back at Hunter long before I found myself involved in discussions on the economic problems of the staff below professorial ranks. Many instructors and other staff members were underpaid and had no security of tenure or promotion. We organized the Hunter College Instructors Association and I became one of the leading forces in it. We won concessions for this group, and I was elected its representative to the faculty council.

The Instructors Association at Hunter was set up so that the two representatives on the faculty would have a guide as to how their colleagues wished them to vote. It was a new type of organization for college teachers — a grass-roots organization for immediate action on important questions of privilege and one in which discussion was uninhibited. Some of the older members of the professorial group were secretly happy to see a rebellious instructors' group give the president a hard time, for there had been a change in that office too: we had a new and different type of president now.

When I first came to college President Davis, the incumbent, was an eminently correct scholar and gentleman. He was a Protestant, tolerant of all and removed from all. The faculty was permitted to do pretty much as they pleased because he and they belonged to a homogeneous group. It was a *laissez-faire* system in which the president selected the heads of departments and they in turn selected their teachers. They were permitted the widest kind of latitude in their personal lives and their methods of teaching. It was the recognized pattern of the liberal arts college of the day.

But President Davis died in the later twenties, and Dr. John Kieran, a kindly old gentleman, who headed the

Department of Education at Hunter was appointed. Dr. Kieran was a Catholic and was regarded by certain members of the faculty as an unfortunate choice for president. But Dr. Kieran had powerful friends in City Hall and the trustees considered him an asset in the constant struggle for the finances which had to be sought from the city budget.

He did not, however, live long enough to make any changes in the administration. When young, vigorous Dr. Eugene Colligan, an Irish Catholic and straight from the public-school system, was chosen to be his successor, there was real consternation among the old guard. Submerged anti-Catholic embers were fanned to flame. The fact that he had come from the administration of a public high school was looked upon as a disaster for the college.

Dr. Colligan misread the nature of the reaction to him. Since he was young and vigorous and happy with his new position, he moved immediately to establish his leadership there, and began bringing in new ideas. But he soon found he was up against a stone wall. His troubles arose not only from the old guard among the faculty but also from the students and from the new type of city politics ushered in in 1932 by the election of Fiorello LaGuardia, which was to New York City what the Roosevelt administration was to the country.

The recognition in 1933 in Washington of the USSR brought a tremendous change in the activities of the communists on our college campus. Recognition brought respectability; it led to the organization of such groups as Friends of the Soviet Union, which was led by engineers and social workers and which soon extended to the world of art and science and to education in general.

At Hunter it brought about a completely changed situation among students, staff, and administration. In our college the initiative was not taken by any of the staff — and this included the younger teachers — for we had no known members of the Communist Party among us. But communist students went into action and before long had a tremendous impact on these same young teachers. One hears a great deal about the influence of teachers on their students. During this early period of communistic influence on the campus Hunter students and City College students had a much greater effect on the teachers.

Almost overnight and seemingly from nowhere organization arose. Groups of the Young Communist League and the League for Industrial Democracy — an organization originating in England among Fabians — appeared in our midst, small dedicated bands of young people. This soon led to mass groups of students who began clamoring for the right to meet on the campus; if permission was not granted, they met outside and protested very loudly.

I was very conscious of one thing: these organizations were not springing up spontaneously; some creating group was behind them. But it was true that the student answer was spontaneous and very immediate. Suddenly there had appeared on the indifferent campus a student group who seemed to care, to believe in things, to be willing to work and suffer for what they believed in and cared for. Before long they had infected the entire student body.

At the time I was deep in the struggle of the instructors for a modicum of economic security, and I felt a great kinship with these students. They were the "depression babies" who were now determined to take matters into their own hands. They were contemptuous of the previous generation which had bequeathed them a legacy of want and depression. They were offered no good hope of future careers. And now, through this new hope that was sweeping the campus, they were going to do something to help themselves.

What they were doing emerged very slowly but it was this: they were unconsciously beginning to ally themselves with the proletariat, with the workers. And from this was born the intellectual proletariat which in the next years was to be the backbone of hundreds of communist organizations — and which was, indeed, to provide active men and women for the mass movements of the next twenty years.

Others had heard of our successful organization of the Instructors Association and we were soon approached by representatives from the other city colleges for help. The result was a committee uniting the efforts of the instructors in all the municipally owned colleges of New York City.

Almost immediately this city-wide group was approached by a group from the private colleges. The approach came through Margaret Schlauch of New York University, who arranged meetings which included representatives of Columbia, Long Island University, and the city colleges. We held many meetings at which we discussed the plight of the intellectuals. The men and women gathered together included many able young people: Howard Selsam, now head of the Jefferson School of Social Science; Margaret Schlauch, today a professor in the University of Cracow; her younger sister Helen who later married Infels (an associate of Albert Einstein) who is also teaching in Poland. Sidney Hook stayed with the group a short while, and then left. Together we planned to form the American Association of University Teachers to fight for the bread-and-butter issues of the lower ranks of college personnel.

For some unknown reason this organization was short-lived. To replace it Margaret Schlauch called together the remnants of the group and proposed a new type of organization. I did not then realize how the wheels within wheels moved but I did feel something new had come into the picture. Strange people were brought to the little gatherings at Margaret's house and though the rest of us were all teachers and college employees, the new figures had nothing to do with the colleges. They began to enlist our group in the struggle against fascism.

To one of the meetings Margaret brought an emaciated woman who talked about the underground movement against fascism. She spoke with an air of authority. Without it Harriet Silverman would have seemed plain to the point of ugliness, but she carried this air of authority like a magic cloak, and it transformed her. She proved a different sort of person from those I had met in organizational work. She talked about the man she called her husband, a man named Engdahl, who was then in Europe to propagandize the Scottsboro Case. Like herself, he was, I learned later, an international agent of the world communist movement.

Harriet singled me out almost from the first. At her invitation I promised to visit her at her home. When she stood up to go I looked at her threadbare tweed coat, her shapeless hat, and I was moved by her evident sense of dedication.

She was the new type of ascetic of our day, a type I was to find prevalent in the Communist Party. She lived in a small remodeled apartment on the East Side and I climbed four steep flights to reach it. The room had a cloistered atmosphere; it was lined with bookshelves on which I noticed Lenin's complete works, Karl Marx, Engels, Stalin, Bimba's *History of the Labor Movement*, and other books on sociology and labor. There was nothing trivial there. I noted no poetry. On one wall hung a large picture of Lenin, draped with Red flags bearing the hammer and sickle.

Harriet was ill the night I visited her. She sat in an old flannel bathrobe and talked with intensity of plans to remake the world. I was impressed by the fact that she was not concerned about her own poverty, and thought only of the working people of the world. Suddenly I felt that my efforts to increase salaries for a few college teachers were insignificant. She made me feel ashamed of having a good job and a comfortable apartment. So moved was I that I pressed on her all the money I had with me.

Harriet suggested that the group of college teachers gathered at Margaret's house should organize an anti-fascist literature committee for the purpose of doing research, writing pamphlets, and raising funds.

She told me frankly she was a Communist. "I'm not afraid of labels," I replied. "I'd join the devil himself to fight fascism."

When I asked Harriet how the money contributed to the anti-fascist cause was distributed, she said, "Through the Party and its contacts."

I may have looked skeptical, for she quickly asked, "Would you like to meet Earl Browder?" I replied in the affirmative, and we made an appointment to meet him the following week at the communist headquarters in Twelfth Street.

When Harriet and I went there we were taken up to the ninth floor in what was more a freight than a passenger elevator. About the whole shabby building I felt the same atmosphere of dedicated poverty that I had found in Harriet in her drab clothes and the drab tenement in which she lived. It was definitely of the people and for the people, I thought.

Earl Browder did not look as I had expected the leader

of the Communist Party to look. With his quiet, thoughtful face and shock of gray hair he was exactly like the popular concept of a professor in a small Midwest college.

We talked about various things — of our anti-fascist committee, its part in the fight against tyranny, of the necessity of being on friendly terms with all nations which opposed fascism. It was a friendly, pleasant talk and when we left, Earl Browder went to the elevator with us, bidding us good-by with a friendly smile.

At the meetings of the Anti-Fascist Literature Committee we knew there were Communists in our midst, but it was considered bad form to ask questions, and they put on an elaborate display of nonpartisanship, perhaps to condition the rest of us. Our committee did write several pamphlets, but the important thing we did was to raise thousands of dollars for the cause and to spread its propaganda.

Little by little the college teachers who came to these increasingly interesting meetings felt the need of a larger dedication. It was a call to action of the innocents — and even today I do not know how many of them were among the innocents.

Sometimes when we grew excited, and when doubts came, Margaret would raise her cool voice, which was as prim and proper as was her D.A.R. background. She could always lessen tension and resolve doubts by some simple remark in her cultivated tones.

To carry out the work of the Anti-Fascist Literature Committee I embarked on a fund-raising campaign supervised by Harriet Silverman. I arranged for meetings and social affairs at my home where we dispensed refreshments and propaganda in return for cash. To these gatherings Harriet began bringing many well-dressed, sophisticated Communists. There were doctors and lawyers and businessmen among our new guests, and there were always a few functionaries of the Party, like Harriet, threadbare and with an ascetic and dedicated air that made the rest of us feel how much more they must be giving than we, the petty bourgeoisie. Other communist types also came, such as men and women in the arts — singers, musicians, dancers, who visited us between acts at night clubs or theaters and added a touch of glamor.

Mingled with these bourgeois elements was another group of Communists who lent a different kind of glamor to the assembled group. These were the real proletarians — longshoremen, painters, plumbers, shipping clerks, and sailors. The young college instructors who were the ostensible sponsors of these meetings were given a feeling of participating with the real forces of life. In this rubbing of elbows of Ph.D.'s and plumbers' helpers there was a leveling of distinctions. The common ground on which we met was that the past of society had been bad, the present was corrupt, and the future would be worth while only if it became collective.

Unemployed councils were being set up on a country-wide basis. In New York the Ex-Servicemen's League, which had organized the bonus march to Washington, was especially active. In working with this group on a program for relief and social security I began to meet some odd and interesting characters.

Perhaps Paddy Whalen best represented the picturesque elements among the Communists of that era. He was a little Irishman, the mayor of Hooversville as they named this town of shanties over on the Jersey flats. He had piercing black eyes. He drank too much and ate too little. In his way, he was dedicated to the labor movement, having once been an IWW, a movement which had supposedly the opposite aims of communism. But in the early thirties all the people who were in unorthodox movements or who had lost their ties with society, whether muckrakers, syndicalists, anarchists, or socialists, were pulled along by the cyclonic fury of the organized communist movement. Without a positive program of their own they were drawn into the vortex of the well-integrated, well-financed movement which was suddenly legalized with the American recognition of the Soviet Union.

Paddy Whalen came from the Middle West. Once a Catholic, he argued doctrine with priests yet begged help for strikers from men of all faiths. As mayor of a pathetic heap of boxes and tins, he wore with great dignity a hand-me-down black derby and an overcoat which reached his heels. At his headquarters he interviewed the press and they found him good copy. Sometimes, I suppose, he put fresh courage in the hearts of his dispossessed citizens. He made them see themselves as a band of Robin Hoods and not as rejected failures.

In the process of preparing a country for revolution the Communist Party tries to enlist the masses. It seeks to enlist the unattached people, for they have little to lose and are the first to capitulate to organized excitement. But to Paddy freedom meant a great deal. He was willing to defend it with his fists. I doubt whether Paddy would long have served the communist world plan of slavery.

I heard one Party leader say of him: "He is a wonderful comrade to help make a revolution but after it is successful we are going to have to kill him because he would immediately proceed to unmake it."

They did not have to kill him; another power did that. When World War II came, Paddy did not seek "union immunity"; he enlisted long before merchant ships had convoys or anti-aircraft guns for defense. His ship went down in burning oil and he with her. How he would have laughed to see the Government, at the insistence of his union and the communist press, name a liberty ship after him! For the Party was able to make use even of his memory to entrap others.

There were many others besides Paddy who were caught up in the Party either from need or desire. They included the unemployed councils, the fighters against fascism, the foreign-born, and the racial and religious minorities who came under its spell. Even today I can understand the attraction it had for the intellectual proletariat. It was as if a great family welcomed them as members.

I often marveled at the sacrifices made by these Communist Party members. In my classes at Hunter were Young Communist Leaguers who would go without lunch to buy paper and ink and other items for propaganda leaflets. Their emaciated faces made my heart ache. Their half-hearted participation in their studies, their frequent cutting of classes, their sacrifice of academic standing to fulfill some task assigned them, were sad to see. I saw college girls exploited by cold Party hacks. They were expendable, and in their places would come other wide-eyed, eager young people with a desire for sacrifice.

I remember especially an Irish "Catholic" girl, an organizer of the unemployed and a leader of mass demonstrations. Helen Lynch was tubercular, but she never stopped working for the Party until she died. Then the Communists claimed her as a martyr.

It was true that it was an infectious thing, this comradeship, for so often it helped in dire need such as Rent Parties where Communists gathered money to pay the rent of some comrade. This sort of personal aid did much to overcome the doctrinaire aridity of orders by the "functionaries," the title given the bureaucrats, the skeleton staff which stands ready to take over when the Revolution comes to pass.

At Hunter I continued active in the Instructors Association to better the economic conditions of the college teachers. Soon I was invited by a number of communist teachers to attend meetings on lower Fifth Avenue where I met top executives of the so-called Class Room Teachers Association. Ostensibly this was a grass-roots movement of teachers, but they were being taught the techniques of mass action and were carefully organized on the basis of the class-struggle philosophy. They were a disciplined band secretly associated with the Trade Union Unity League led by William Z. Foster.

The Class Room Teachers had two tasks: to convert a considerable number of teachers to a revolutionary approach to problems, and to recruit for the Communist Party as many members as possible. Some of these teachers were also members of the Teachers Union Local 5 of the American Federation of Teachers and therein they formed an organized minority opposition to the prevailing non-communist leadership.

Like all Red unions of the early thirties, the Class Room Teachers Association helped give publicity to the bread-and-butter problems acute at the time. There were many unemployed teachers in the city and a large number of substitute teachers who were hired by the Board of Education at a low daily wage year in and year out. On such issues the Red organization capitalized while the conservative organizations were too inept to act.

The Class Room Teachers sent mass delegations to the Board of Education. It issued attacks against the officials of the city and jibed at the then-respectable Teachers Union under the leadership of Lefkowitz and Linville. Teachers such as Celia Lewis, Clara Rieber, and Max Diamond emerged as leaders of the Red minority within the A. F. of L. Teachers Union. By organizing the unemployed teachers and fighting to have them in the Union, it became clear that before long the Teachers Union would be controlled by the Reds.

I did not become a Communist overnight. It came a little at a time. I had been conditioned by my education and association to accept this materialistic philosophy. Now came new reasons for acceptance. I was grateful for communist support in the struggles of the Instructors Association. I admired the selfless dedication of many who belonged to the Party. They took me into their fraternal circle and made me feel at home. I was not interested in any long-range Party objectives but I did welcome their assistance on immediate issues, and I admired them for their courage. Most of all I respected the way they fought for the forgotten man of the city. So I did not argue with them about the "dictatorship of the proletariat" which they talked about, or about its implications.

Of course some of my friends were unhappy about my new course. One day when Ruth Goldstein and I were walking down Sixty-eighth Street she spoke bitterly about my new affiliations.

"You are getting too involved, Bella," she said. "You will get hurt. Wait and see!"

I laughed at her. "Oh, Ruth, you are too concerned about promotions and tenures. There are other things in life."

"What about this one-party system that they favor?" she demanded.

"Well, you know we really have only a one-party system in America right now," I retorted. "Remember the Harvard professor who says that both political parties resemble empty bottles with different labels?"

Ruth continued arguing and I finally said: "Oh, Ruth, I am only interested in the present. What the Communist Party says about the future is not important to me. The sanity of the American people will assert itself. But these people are about the only ones who are doing anything about the rotten conditions of today. That is why I am with them, and," I ended truculently, "I will stay with them."

Of course I was not the only American who thought one could go along with the good things the Communists did and then reject their objectives. It was a naïve idea and many of us were naïve. It took a long time for me to know that once you march with them there is no easy return. I learned over the years that if you stumbled from weariness they had no time to pick up a fallen comrade. They simply marched over him.

The saddest situation I saw in the Party were the hundreds of young people eager to be used. And the Party did use this mass of anonymous people for its immediate purposes. And so young people were burned out before they could reach maturity. But I saw, too, how inexhaustible was the supply of human beings willing to be sacrificed. Much of the strength of the Party, of course, is derived from this very ruthlessness in exploiting people.

On various occasions I was approached to join the Party as a regular member. When I agreed to do so I learned to my surprise that Harriet Silverman had put a stop to it. I was her contact; she said she had taken the matter up with "the center" and it was decided I was not to join. I must not be seen at secret Party gatherings. Harriet would give me Marxist literature and my instructions. I was not to be known as a Communist.

I had never indulged in double dealing. It seemed to me that if I agreed with the Party the best way to show it was by joining it. However, I reluctantly accepted discipline. Since I knew something of the struggle to organize the labor movement in America, by analogy the Party began to represent in my thinking an organization of workers who were likewise being hounded by men of wealth and power.

74

I could not at that time know, as I did later, how men of wealth use the communist movement to bend workers to their will. So I quite willingly adopted the clichés about secrecy being necessary because of the brutality and savagery of the working-class enemies. I soon learned that the members exposed to the public were not the important Communists.

Harriet consoled me about my status in relation to the Party, saying I must be saved for real tasks and must not at this time be exposed. So I became not a member of an idealistic group of which I was proud, but the tool of a secret, well-organized world power. Harriet brought me literature, took the financial contributions I collected, gave me orders.

One day I ran by chance into one of our neighbors, Christopher McGrath, now the Surrogate of Bronx County. I remembered him as a boy on our street who had pulled my hair when I was a child. At the time of this chance meeting he was married and was chairman of the Education Committee of the Assembly for that year.

We chatted about old times, and I asked his aid with our instructors. He was willing to help. Of course he knew nothing of my communist sympathy. Next day at his office we drafted a bill on college teachers' tenure which he promised to introduce the following Monday night.

I was surprised at the speed of this and even more at the speed with which word of the bill got around the Hunter College campus. Soon afterward I was called down to President Colligan's office and learned that our bill had given tenure to everybody on the staff except the President!

We reworked the bill and eventually the new form satisfied the President, too, and now included professors, instructors, and other college personnel. But the interesting thing was the way I was now looked up to on my campus.

In those days teachers were far removed from the legislative process and knew little of it and regarded it as a beneficent kind of black magic.

The fight to pass this bill gave new impetus to the city-wide organizations of college teachers. I had some stormy sessions in my home with communist representatives from the three city colleges. We argued until late into the night about amendments. This matter of having to argue with pettifogging perfectionists was to become a common experience in communist life; reports and resolutions were always prepared by a group and the comrades fought over each word so as to achieve an exactitude of political expression.

However, as a result of our combined efforts, the tenure bill was passed and the joint Instructors Associations held a victory luncheon at the Fifth Avenue Hotel. The bill was signed in due course by Governor Lehman.

I now found myself regarded as a legislative expert. My success served to catapult me into a new post, that of legislative representative of the Teachers Union Local 5. I was now an officer of an A.F. of L. union and for this reason more important to the Party.

CHAPTER SEVEN

In the spring of 1936 I got a six-month leave of absence from the College to serve as the legislative representative of the Teachers Union. I spent much of my time in Albany, in Washington, and at City Hall in New York. I was successful in having two Union bills passed and the Union was well pleased.

I now represented a growing educational pressure group. With the Communists in control, the New York Teachers Union expanded its membership rolls by taking in unemployed teachers, substitute teachers, and WPA teachers. These made a large bloc for political pressure. We added further strength to it by working with the communist section of the PTA and several student organizations.

With these to support campaigns, my activity in politics was greatly increased. I organized this bloc on an assembly-district basis with teacher-union captains in charge of each district. When legislation was pending, I called on my own captains to put pressure on recalcitrant representatives.

The Communist Party was pleased, and later it promoted to important positions with the American Labor Party, which it controlled, many of the teachers who got their first experience in practical politics with teachers' district clubs.

At this time I became one of the Teachers Union delegates to the A.F. of L. Central Trades and Labor Council of New York. When I first went to Beethoven Hall on East Fifth Street, Joseph Ryan was president and George Meany was legislative representative.

I was proud of the assignment. I was young and idealistic and eager to serve the workers. I now became a member of the Communist Party "fraction" in the A.F. of L. This meant that I would meet regularly with the Communist Party members of the A.F. of L. and the leaders of the Party in order to push A.F. of L. policy toward the communist line.

The Party maintained an active fraction in labor groups, including the A.F. of L. In 1934 the Red unions under the title TUUL, led by William Z. Foster, had been ordered liquidated by the Communist International. The radicalized core of workers, trained by Foster, turned their energies to A.F. of L. unions. They attracted new followers by militant support of legislation for the unemployed. This struggle for a worthy cause enabled the Party to build emotional and organizational ties with workers belonging to many unions.

In 1936 I met, through the Party, committees of the striking seamen who, under the leadership of the Communist Party, were fighting both the shipowners and the corrupt leadership of the old I.S.U., an affiliate of the A.F. of L. A rank-and-file movement was organized against the old leadership of the I.S.U. These insurgents were led by Joseph Curran and Blackie Myers, who immediately

78

started a strike, unauthorized by their union, against the shipowners. To gain some support from organized labor they sought assistance from the Central Trades and Labor Council. They wanted to present their grievances before delegates of the city's organized labor body.

I was summoned by the Communist Party and told I had been selected to present to the Central Trades a petition of the striking seamen with their demands for a reorganization of their union along democratic lines. I agreed to cooperate though I was only partly aware of the implications. I met the committee of seamen outside Beethoven Hall. Joseph Curran and a number of other seamen gave me the petition and briefed me.

There was full attendance inside the hall; the leadership expected trouble. When the agenda of the meeting had been covered, I asked for recognition from Joe Ryan and got the floor. To disarm the opposition I talked first about democracy in unions and then I announced breathlessly:

"I hereby present the petition of the striking seamen. In the interest of union democracy they are entitled to a hearing."

Pandemonium broke loose. The chairman hit his gavel again and again, so hard that it finally flew from his fingers. That night I was escorted home by a group of the communist delegates who feared I might suffer bodily harm. But the press got the story of the seamen's demands and printed it. We had accomplished our mission.

I learned something important that night. I found that acts of daring, supported by the appearances of moral justification, have a terrific impact in building a movement, regardless of whether or not you win. This is a fact the Communists know how to use.

Of course I was hardly representing the teachers by becoming involved in matters which were of no immediate concern to my union. But I had learned that serving the Communist Party was the first requisite for continued leadership in my union.

From my tutors in the Party I learned many communist lessons. I learned that Lenin held in contempt unions interested only in economic betterment of workers, because he held that the liberation of the working class would not come through reforms. I learned that unions which followed a reformist policy were guilty of the Marxist crime of "economism." I learned that trade unions are useful only insofar as they could be used politically to win worker acceptance of the theory of class struggle and to convince workers that their only hope of improving their conditions is in revolution.

Again and again I heard Jack Stachel and Foster and lesser Communist Party labor leaders repeat that American workers need to be "politicalized" and "proletarianized." Their feeling was that the American worker was not conscious of his class role because he was too comfortable. In line with this I saw senseless strikes called or prolonged. At first I did not understand the slogan frequently proclaimed by these men: "Every defeat is a victory." Loss of salary, or position, or even loss of life was not important as long as it brought the worker to acceptance of the class struggle.

That year I was elected as delegate to the State Federation of Labor convention at Syracuse. The Communists and some of the liberal unions were determined to pass a resolution endorsing the formation of a Labor Party. I attended the Communist Party fraction meeting in New York in preparation for this convention. We went over the resolutions to be introduced and the objectives to be achieved. Assignments were made to individual delegates.

This use of fractions made the Communist Party effective in noncommunist groups. They went prepared, organized, trained, and disciplined with a program worked out in detail, and before other groups had a chance to think the Communists were winning advantages. They worked in every convention as an organized bloc. In other organized blocs the Communists had "sleepers," assigned to protect Communist Party interests. These "sleepers" were active members in noncommunist blocs for the purpose of hamstringing and destroying the power of the opposition.

The "progressive" bloc at the State Federation convention that year decided to run me for a position in the State Federation of Labor. It seems ridiculous to me now that one so newly come to the labor movement should have been pushed forward against the established machine. But this, too, was a communist tactic, for Communists have no hesitation whatever in bringing unknown people forward into leadership, the more callow or ill-equipped the better, since they will therefore more easily be guided by the Party. The weaker they are, the more certainly they will carry out the Party's wishes. Suddenly and dramatically the Communist Party makes somebodies out of nobodies. If tactics change, they also drop them just as quickly and the somebodies again become nobodies.

By 1936 plans had already been made by important forces in Washington for the launching of the American Labor Party, presumably as a method of solidifying the labor vote in New York for President Roosevelt. The Communists pledged their total support. Of course, no one in his right mind expected the A.F. of L. to move as a bloc into an independent labor party. The purpose was to radicalize the workers of New York and paralyze the two major parties. As I saw it the struggle on the floor of the

81

State Federation convention was to launch the idea of a Labor Party to "politicalize" labor unions by tying them to a party presumably of their own as does the British Labor Party.

My nomination for office in the state A.F. of L. gave me an opportunity to make a passionate plea for independent political action by organized labor. It was well received. Though I was defeated, as the Communists had expected, I received considerable support. I got the vote not only of the communist delegates but also of many of the representatives of liberal unions.

It did not matter to the Party leader, who masterminded this activity from a hotel room at the convention, that I was fearful my action might result in reprisals against the Teachers Union which desperately needed A.F. of L. support. Ours was a union without job control and our activities were limited to pleading our cause for salaries and working conditions before city and state legislative bodies. We depended on support from organized labor to achieve our program.

In 1936 the communist hold on the A.F. of L. in New York State was slim. The Party was afraid to expose well-placed comrades in the A.F. of L. apparatus, reserving them for key positions in vital industries and for long-range strategy. In addition there were Communists occupying important positions in the unions who enjoyed their union "pie card" positions, and they objected to being sacrificed even by the Party. These argued that it was more important for them to hold their positions than to be used for mere opposition purposes.

The leadership of the Teachers Union was not affected by a fear of losing jobs; the tenure law for public schoolteachers was now effective. Therefore, the Party leaders found it expedient to use the teacher leaders in the A.F.

of L. as the spearhead of A.F. of L. work. In addition teachers were generally better informed about current Party writings and were better disposed to follow the Party line than the old-time communist union leaders who were hampered by the fact that they had to give consideration to the bread-and-butter issues for their unions. Then, too, the teacher representatives were not affected by a desire to preserve "pie card" positions since there was no material advantage to leadership in the Teachers Union in my day.

But this steady use of the Teachers Union by the Communist Party in the city, in the state, and at times even in the national A.F. of L. brought reprisals from A.F. of L. leaders. They became colder and more unwilling to accede to requests for assistance from the Teachers Union.

When I appeared in Albany in the fall of 1936 as the legislative representative of the Teachers Union, I found I had a hard time ahead of me.

Dr. Lefkowitz, who had represented the Union for many years, was bitter over being replaced by a neophyte who was doing the bidding of the Communist Party. I found that he had prepared for my appearance by announcing to everyone that I was a Communist and he had warned the legislators against co-operating with me.

I went to the A.F. of L. legislative office on South Hawk Street to talk with Mr. Hanley, but Dr. Lefkowitz had been there before me. I was met with stony politeness. I again wondered why there should be such bitter feeling about the control of a relatively small organization; its total membership in 1936 was under three thousand. I was to learn in the years to come that those who seek to influence public opinion on any question are just as effective with a small as with a large organization; and that it is easier to control a small organization.

I made overtures to the leader of the Joint Committee

of Teachers Organizations, the conservative association of the New York City teachers. May Andres Healey knew the New York schools and the New York political scene. She was endowed with political shrewdness. When I went to see her she expressed herself in no uncertain terms about the Teachers Union. She did not believe in unions for teachers, she said briefly. It was too bad to have her against me, for though she was not part of the A.F. of L., she had strong connections with their city and state leadership.

We did not receive the wholehearted support of the A.F. of L. because the Teachers Union in America was basically pro-socialist and supported an educational system intended to prepare children for the new economic collectivist system which we regarded as inevitable. This went far beyond A.F. of L. policy of those days.

Though I was at a decided disadvantage in Albany, I was not easily discouraged. I had a "good" legislative program and the Party comrades had assured me they did not expect me to get passed the bills we were sponsoring. Their real purpose was to have the program popularized and to use this as a means of recruiting more teachers into the Union.

I set to work with a will. I cultivated assemblymen and senators. I studied their districts and learned what problems faced them in elections. I held meetings with voters in their districts. I made many friends among the legislators.

In the fall of that year I went back to my classes at Hunter. By the following spring I asked for another leave of absence, but this time I had to appeal to Mayor Fiorello LaGuardia to intervene for me with the Board of Trustees to obtain it. The Mayor was a friend of mine and at that time willing to indulge me.

In the May Day parade of 1936 more than five hundred teachers marched with the Communists. These included many college teachers. I was one of them. I had, in fact, been selected to lead the teacher contingent.

I felt excited as I marched with segments of organized labor. This was my gesture of defiance against greed and corruption. It was also an affirmation of my belief that a better world could be created.

Gone now was the pain which had moved me in the earlier years of the 1930's, when I saw crowds of white-faced people standing in front of the closed doors of the Bowery Savings Bank. Gone was the shame I felt when I saw well-bred men furtively pick up cigarette butts from city streets or when I saw soup lines at the mission doors.

In 1936 people had a little more money than in those tragic years of 1932 to 1934. On the whole a tremendous change had taken place in America. Millions of people formerly regarded as middle class found themselves on relief or on WPA and had been merged into the comrade-ship of the dispossessed. To people of this group the Communist Party brought psychological support. It saved their pride by blaming the economic system for their troubles and it gave them something to hate. It also made it possible for them to give expression to that hate by defiance.

Many of these new proletarians marched that May Day down Eighth Avenue, through streets lined with slum buildings, singing, "Arise, ye prisoners of starvation, Arise, ye wretched of the earth," and ending with the promise, "Ye have been naught. Ye shall be all." These men and women who marched were drawn together by a sense of loss and a fear of future insecurity.

When the parade disbanded, the college teachers, jubi-lant because of this mingling with proletarian comrades, gathered at a beer garden where we drank beer and sang again the songs of the workers. We college teachers had come a long way by marching in a Communist May Day parade. We felt part of something new and alive.

With the others I went from one group to another that evening. By the early morning we had reached one of the intimate little night clubs which the Communist Party financed and where Party people were wont to congregate. We were tired by that time and willing to listen to entertainers in the club.

When the paying patrons had gone, we continued our own celebration. We were a mixed group — workers being groomed by the Party as labor leaders, intellectuals, men and women of the middle class who were beginning to identify themselves with the proletariat. Only emotion could have bound us together, for our group embraced serious workers with good jobs as well as crackpots and psychopaths and some of life's misfits.

Beginning in 1936 a prodigious effort was made by the Party in support of the Spanish Civil War, and this continued until 1939. Perhaps no other activity aroused greater devotion among American intellectuals.

Since 1932 the Communist Party had publicized itself as the leading opponent of fascism. It had used the emotional appeal of anti-fascism to bring many people to the acceptance of communism, by posing communism and fascism as alternatives. Its propaganda machine ground out an endless stream of words, pictures, and cartoons. It played on intellectual, humanitarian, racial, and religious sensibilities until it succeeded to an amazing degree in conditioning America to recoil at the word fascist even when people did not know its meaning.

Today I marvel that the world communist movement was able to beat the drums against Germany and never once betray what the inner group knew well: that some of the same forces which gave Hitler his start had also started Lenin and his staff of revolutionists from Switzerland to St. Petersburg to begin the revolution which was to result in the Soviet totalitarian state.

There was not a hint that despite the propaganda of hate unleashed against Germany and Italy, communist representatives were meeting behind the scenes to do business with Italian and German fascists to whom they sold matériel and oil. There was not a hint that Soviet brass was meeting with German brass to redraw the map of Europe. There was no betrayal of these facts until one day they met openly to sign a contract for a new map of Europe — a treaty made by Molotov and Von Ribbentrop.

In the Spanish Civil War, the Party called upon its many members in the field of public relations, agents who made their living by writing copy for American business, for the sale of soap, whisky, and cigarettes. They gave the Party tremendous assistance in conditioning the mind of America. People of all ranks joined the campaign for the Loyalists: pacifists, humanitarians, political adventurers, artists, singers, actors, teachers, and preachers. All these and more poured their best efforts into this campaign.

During the Spanish War the Communist Party was able to use some of the best talent of the country against the Catholic Church by repeating ancient appeals to prejudice and by insinuating that the Church was indifferent to the poor and was against those who wanted only to be free.

The communist publicists carefully took for their own the pleasant word of Loyalist and called all who opposed them "Franco-Fascists." This was a literary *coup* which confused many men and women. Violent communist literature repeatedly lumped all of the Church hierarchy on the side of the "Fascists," and, using this technique, they sought to destroy the Church by attacking its priests. This was not a new tactic. I had seen it used in our own country over and over again. When the Communists organized Catholic workers, Irish and Polish and Italian, in labor unions they always drove a wedge between lay Catholics and the priests, by flattering the laity and attacking the priests.

In the Spanish campaign the Communists in the United States followed Moscow directives. They were the distant outpost of the Soviet realm and co-ordinated with the Communist International in details. When the call came to organize the American contingent of the International Brigade, the communist port agents of the National Maritime Union along the East Coast provided false passports and expedited the sending of this secret army to a friendly country.

Various unions were combed for members who would join the Abraham Lincoln Brigade which was the American division of the International Brigade. The Communists used the prestige of Lincoln's name as they had other patriots' names to stir men's souls for propaganda purposes.

I, myself, swallowed the Party's lies on the Spanish Civil War. There was little forthcoming from American national leaders to expose this fraud. The Party, from time to time, produced a few poor, bewildered Spanish priests who, we were told, were Loyalists and these were publicized as the "People's priests" as against the others, the Fascists. In retrospect it is easy to see how completely they twisted the American's love of freedom and justice to win emotional support for the Soviet adventure in Spain.

Through numerous committees the Communist Party raised thousands of dollars for its Spanish campaign. But the tremendous advertising campaign could not have been financed from the contributions made at mass meetings and other gatherings, though these were not small sums. I remember one mass meeting (where I made the speech), held under the auspices of the Teachers Union. It netted more than twelve thousand dollars.

It became obvious, as the extensive campaign went on, that some of the funds were coming from sources other than the collections. It is now well known that the Soviet Union was doing everything in its power to bring the foreign policy of the United States into conformity with its own devious plans and that it did not hesitate to use trickery to do so. It wanted the United States to support Soviet policy on Spain. I did not understand this at the time. After that odd pieces of information and desultory recollections of events stayed in my mind and finally pieced out an understandable picture.

As one example of the puzzle that finally became a picture there is the story of the *Erica Reed,* which will serve as an example of hundreds of others. It was supposed to be a mercy ship taking food, milk, and medicines to hard-pressed Barcelona. It was chartered ostensibly by the North American Committee for Loyalist Spain. In reality it was financed by Soviet agents.

The *Erica Reed* was laid up in New Orleans. At that time anti-communists were in control of the National Maritime Union in the Gulf, and the ship was manned by a crew which was either anti-communist or nonpolitical. This did not fit into the plans of the Soviet agent and the American Communists working with him. So it was decided to bring the *Erica Reed* to New York and there replace her crew with trusted Party men.

The little Soviet agent in a rumpled suit who sat in a New York hotel with several Communists from the National Maritime Union, and with Roy Hudson, then the Party whip on the water front, excitedly peeled off hundred-dollar bills from a huge wad and insisted that a trustworthy crew be placed on the *Erica Reed,* even if the old crew had to be removed by force and hospitalized.

Later, I talked to one of the men assigned to switch crews. A group had been ordered to board the vessel at night. Armed with blackjacks and lead pipes, they set to work. Some of the crew suffered broken jaws, arms, and legs, and, as the little Soviet agent had planned, some were hospitalized. In addition a crowd of boys from the fur market, who were told they must fight fascism, congregated near the East Side pier where the ship was docked. They attacked the members of the crew who escaped the goon squad on the ship. They did not know that they were assaulting fellow Americans and were confused as to what the fracas was about.

Only the captain, an old Scandinavian, remained of the original crew. The new crew signed on by the New York office of the Union were nearly all pro-communist sailors, some of whom were looking for an opportunity for violent action and adventure.

When the *Erica Reed* left Sandy Hook, customs inspectors swarmed over her. But they found no arms or ammunition, and left the ship with only one bit of contraband: a communist blonde who was determined to go to Spain, and who was removed from the cabin of the chief engineer.

When the *Erica Reed* cleared Gibraltar and nosed toward her destination, Franco's gunboats ordered her to stop. The captain, concerned for the safety of his vessel, made ready to do so. As he turned to give the order, a communist member of the crew held a pistol to the captain's head and commanded, "Proceed to Barcelona."

The Spanish gunboat, reluctant to seize a ship flying the American flag, returned to headquarters for further instructions. The "relief ship" with its supplies reached Barcelona where she was immediately ordered to Odessa. And so the *Erica Reed*, ostensibly chartered by the North American Committee for Loyalist Spain, was sent to Odessa by her real charterer, the Soviet Union. The Spanish people were expendable.

During those years house parties were held by our union members to raise money for Loyalist Spain. Union and nonunion teachers were invited. Communists and noncommunists rubbed shoulders and drank cocktails together. Eyes grew moist as the guests were told of bombs dropped on little children in Bilboa.

The International Brigade was eulogized by many Americans. They failed to realize that the first international army under Soviet leadership had been born; that though all the national subdivisions had *national* commissars, these were under *Soviet* commissars! There was the Lincoln Brigade and the Garibaldi Brigade. There was the emerging world military communist leadership developing in Spain. There was Thompson for the United States, Tito for Yugoslavia, André Marty for France, and others to act as the new leaders in other countries.

We teachers recruited soldiers for the Lincoln Brigade. I learned that Sid Babsky, a teacher of the fifth grade in Public School Number 6 in the Bronx who had been a classmate of mine at law school, was among the first to go. He did not return. Ralph Wardlaw, son of a Georgian minister, suddenly left his classes at City College and, without even packing his clothes, left for Spain. Six weeks later we received word of his death. Some of our substitute teachers enlisted and were spirited away to Soviet agents who got them out of the country with or without passports. In Paris they went to a certain address and there were directed across the border.

During this time communist girls wore gold liberty bells inscribed "Lincoln Brigade," as a symbol of their pride in those "fighting fascism." One of our talented Teachers Union members wrote a marching song which we sang at our meetings:

> Abraham Lincoln lives again.
> Abraham Lincoln marches.
> Up tall he stands and his great big hand
> Holds a gun.
> With the Lincoln Battalion behind him,
> He fights for the freedom of Spain.

And at various social affairs we also sang *"Non Pasaron"*; and sometimes with fists closed and lifted we shouted the German International brigade song, *"Freiheit."*

CHAPTER EIGHT

FROM 1936 TO 1938 I was involved in so many activities I had little time for my family and old friends. I devoted myself more and more to the new friends who shared my fanatical sense of dedication. I found little time to read anything except Party literature. This was necessary to hold leadership in a union where many of the leaders were trained and established Communists.

The Teachers Union was growing rapidly in numbers and influence. The college teachers in the Union grew so numerous that a separate local with a separate office was established for them, Local 537. Together with the WPA Local Number 453, our membership grew to almost nine thousand and we extended control to many upstate locals. At its peak the Union boasted ten thousand members, and in it the Communist Party had a fraction of close to a thousand. Among them were Moscow-trained teachers and men and women who had attended the sixth World Congress of the Comintern.

The president of the Union, Charles J. Hendley, a history teacher at George Washington High School, was not a Communist. He was a militant socialist and did not join the Communist Party until he retired from the school system. He then became associated with the *Daily Worker*. He was, however, willing to join with the Communists in the many and varied campaigns of the Teachers Union and of the labor movement generally. He grew to like many of the Communist Party leaders in the Union and that tended to minimize political differences. He was a lonely man; the Union and its leadership were his family and his social life.

The Party left nothing to chance. When in 1936 Lefkowitz and Linville left the Teachers Union because the Communists had control, the Party immediately suggested a candidate for office manager, and Dorothy Wallas, a brassy and pleasant blonde, was placed there to insure Party control, and especially control of the president.

Mr. Hendley carried a full program as a teacher and had little time to give to office detail, but the efficient Miss Wallas was always at hand. He grew fond of her and relied more and more on her judgment, not knowing, of course, that she was a Party member. Miss Wallas meantime used her position as palace favorite to run the office as she saw fit, and, since Mr. Hendley was at school all day, she began to make important decisions.

I was seldom in the Union office. I was at Albany, or out of town organizing, or at City Hall, or at the Board of Education. But to be effective in the Union I found I had to give some consideration to the inner-office politics and I soon learned that Miss Wallas was an inner wheel functioning smoothly. She and I did not clash because I did not want a road block in my relations with Mr. Hendley. As I had often heard her criticize the Communists, I was convinced that she was not one.

94

There was another group at the office, a rigidly communist puritanical group, old-time leaders of the fraction. The thirty or so who made up this group had known each other for years. They had led the struggle against Linville and Lefkowitz. Some had the blessings of Moscow and they were a sort of elite corps, disciplined and unbending except when the Party spoke.

There was a subtle struggle for leadership between this inner core and myself. My strength in any controversy lay in the fact that the Party was using me in labor, legislative, and peace campaigns and that I was used in key positions in labor politics. This gave me prestige which I used to keep the life of the Union from freezing into a rigid communist pattern. I deferred to them often, however, and was firm only when it came to Union policy on the economic interests of the teachers and the need to gain political respect for the Union.

The Party literature of the period was stressing the increasing importance of united fronts for peace, against fascism, against discrimination, against economic insecurity. Earl Browder and other Party leaders were warning Union leaders not to regard Marxism as dogmatic, but as flexible in meeting new situations. As a matter of fact, this literature sometimes seemed a handicap, cluttered as it was with double talk used purposely by Marx and Lenin. Browder emphasized the importance of relying on Stalin who was building socialism in Russia, and only on Stalin because of his shrewdness in dealing with all, even with enemies of the working class, such as English and American capitalists.

We who were the leaders of the united-front period used to shake our heads at the old guard in the Union and scornfully call them Nineteen Fivers, referring to the Russian Revolution of 1905. Yet I see now that this old guard with its endless disputation gave stability to Party control of our Union. It was their whole life; few got anything for their endless hours of work except the right to control. They were dour people though, and some of them, such as Celia Lewis and Clara Rieber, were so dedicated that they were intolerant of anyone's opinions except the opinions of those on their side. I never saw them laugh and I doubt if they knew how.

We had one man in the Union who was so talented in manipulation that he was regarded as the Stalin of the Union — Dale Zysman, also known as Jack Hardy. He had been to Moscow. He had written *The First American Revolution,* thus implying that a greater one was to come. A junior high-school teacher, he was a tall, personable young man with a keen interest in baseball and he held his pipe in his mouth at exactly the angle Stalin did his. The communist fraction had installed him officially as vice-president of the Teachers Union and also unofficially as the arbiter in all disputes between Party members and groups. He also established contacts with non-Party personalities for possible work in the Union. It was he who tried to give the Union Executive Board a well-balanced appearance by persuading Protestant and Catholic teachers to accept posts on the Board where most of the members were communist atheists.

Dale also maintained an espionage system which brought back information on what was going on in the Union as well as in the inner circles of other teachers' organizations. Those who worked in this espionage system, particularly in other left-wing groups, became twisted personalities. Dale, I learned later, reported directly to "Chester," a man I was to know as the chief of the Party's intelligence service.

Later I ran into a real problem with Dale and our blond office manager. Dorothy was making my position with Mr.

96

Hendley difficult by false stories about me. I could not spend hours in the office just to counteract office intrigue. I got nowhere when I took the matter to Dale. But one day two bookkeepers brought me evidence of financial irregularities. They did not want to take it to Mr. Hendley because Miss Wallas was involved. I took this up with Dale and got a brushoff.

Then one day the mystery cleared. We learned that Miss Wallas was not only a good Communist but that she was also Dale's sister! It explained much, and I thought it should be taken up with the leaders of the fraction. But when I stated my discovery and looked at Celia and Clara and the others to get their reactions it was clear from their faces they had known it all the time. I was the one kept in the dark. Miss Wallas was soon afterward sent elsewhere and I was free to carry on my work; but for some time I was unnerved by this duplicity.

Attending conventions took much of my time. No convention of teachers in the United States ever went unnoticed by the Communist Party. The national office would call the leaders of the teacher Communists and discuss with us the nature of the organization and inquire if we had Party members in it. If we had, we would decide which resolutions they were to introduce and which they were to oppose. If we had no members, observers would be sent to make contacts. Particular attention was given to pushing federal aid to the public-education program and to the issue of separation of church and state at these conventions.

We also carefully prepared for meetings of learned societies, such as mathematics and modern-language associations, and those composed of professors of physics, history, and social studies. A careful search of Party members and friends of the Party was made, as well as of

97

liberals and special-interest groups. This was all done months in advance. Then a campaign began to get certain people elected or to have them volunteer to go to a convention so that we would have a core of dependables. Finally we drew up a plan of action to put through certain measures and to try to defeat others.

We felt it was important at these meetings of learned societies to defeat everything which did not conform to Marxist ideology. The result was that the ideology of many of our learned societies has within the last thirty years been deeply affected. The Communists establish a fraction in such societies and whenever possible a leadership for a materialistic, collectivistic, international class-struggle approach.

The conventions were invaluable in bringing together the growing group of scholars who were not members of the Party but who followed Marxist ideology idealistically. For the strength of the Party was increasing in high positions; and job getting and job promotions are a *sine qua non* of academic gatherings. Men are drawn where power is, and these academic men were no different in that respect from traveling salesmen. The Party and its friends were assiduous in developing the job-getting and job-giving phase of these meetings.

At the end of a convention they returned with lists of new conquests, the names of men and women who would go along with us. These names were given to the district organizer of the Party in the locality where each professor lived. The organizer would visit and try to deepen the ideological conquest by flattering his victim, disclosing to him new vistas of usefulness, and by introducing him to an interesting social life. The methods were many; the end was one — a closer tie to the Party.

Before long a professor would become involved in the

proletarian class struggle. His name would then be used to support communist public declaration on national or international policies. Soon the professor identified himself with a "side," and all the good people were on his side and all the greedy, the degraded, the stupid were on the other. Soon he began talking of "our people" and thinking himself part of an unnumbered army of justice marching to a brave new world, or, as one French intellectual Communist, who lost his life in the Resistance, put it, toward "singing tomorrows."

American Federation of Teachers conventions were held during the summer months so teacher delegates could attend without having to leave their classes or to get special permission. This Federation was unique in American education in that it was the only teachers' association organized on a union basis.

The history of the plan for affiliating teachers with labor is interesting. It was first tried in 1902 in San Antonio where a charter was issued directly by the A.F. of L. Later the same year the Chicago Teachers Federation, organized in 1897, affiliated itself with the Chicago Federation of Labor to get labor support for a salary fight with the "vested interests." Many prominent Chicagoans, among them Jane Addams, urged the teachers to affiliate with labor.

A debate raged in educational periodicals as to the advisability of teachers unionizing, a debate which has gone on ever since. By 1916 twenty teachers' organizations in ten different states had affiliated with labor. Some were short-lived, due to local suppression, or to loss of interest, after the immediate objective was won.

In 1916 a call was issued by the Chicago Teachers Union to all locals affiliated with labor. A meeting was held and the American Federation of Teachers, a national organization, was founded. The next month it affiliated with the A.F. of L. with eight charter locals in Chicago, Gary, New York City, Scranton, and Washington, D.C., with a combined membership of twenty-eight hundred. The *American Teacher,* a magazine published by a group of individuals in the New York union, was endorsed as the official publication. At first hostile, boards of education exercised pressure against the new teachers' organization, but by 1920 there were one hundred and forty locals and a membership of twelve thousand.

The American Federation of Teachers in the beginning was sparked by socialists. Its growth was due to the anti-war principles of the American socialists, for there was need of an organization to help teachers involved in the anti-war struggle. Even then most of the members were not socialists but were attracted by the Federation program for economic and social aid. By 1927 the Federation had declined in membership and prestige because of attacks on organized labor. With the coming of the depression it again began to grow and by 1934 there were seventy-five locals in good standing with an active membership of almost ten thousand.

By that time the Communists were displacing the socialists from posts of radical leadership in unions. The steady march of the Communists into the Federation at this period was planned and not accidental. Since twenty-five teachers could form a local and send delegates to the national convention, the communist district organizers began promoting the organizing of teachers, and these began to send delegates, often charming and persuasive ones.

Many of the teachers were not interested in the political struggle in the Federation and did not care to go as delegates. Even in the New York local in my time it was difficult to get non-Party people to go as delegates because the Federation did not pay expenses. But the keenest competition existed among Party members. The communist fraction within the Federation drew up its list carefully and it was considered a mark of honor for Party members or fellow travelers to be selected.

Of course, from 1936 to 1938 our delegation from Local 5 to Federation conventions had to be divided between the communist group which was in control and the opposition which consisted of socialist splinter groups. The struggle between these groups was carried to the national conventions, often to the consternation of the political innocents who still believed that all American politics was ruled by the Republican and the Democratic parties. They could not understand the bitterness, the vituperation, and sometimes the terror which their colleagues exhibited. But one fact was clear to others: the conventions of the Federation became battles for the capture of the minds and the votes of the independent delegates.

My first federation convention was in Philadelphia in 1936. Since it was close to New York City, we were able to send a full quota of delegates while many of the out-of-town locals were forced to send only token representation. To make matters worse we had impressed on the members of the New York fraction that even if they were not delegates they would be needed to entertain and lobby with delegates from other sections. We were so well organized that we were in almost complete control. The arrangements were in the hands of the Philadelphia local, itself communist led and controlled. The party assigned its ablest trades-union functionaries to hold continuous secret sessions in a room at the convention hotel to aid comrades on all questions.

If I had not yet been convinced that the road to progress

was the one pointed out by the Communists, I was certainly overwhelmed by the sense of power which this convention manifested. To it came professors whose names I had read in academic literature and in the press. There was a wide range of delegates, from university men and women of distinction and old-time classroom teachers with the staid dignity that seemed so much a part of the profession in America to the young substitute and unemployed teachers who eyed their situation with economic fear and political and philosophical defiance. There was also the WPA troop, an assortment of men and women who were called teachers but many of whom had been shifted into this category because they were on relief, or had a college education, or some talent that allowed them to be called teachers, such as teaching tap dancing or hairdressing.

A great leveling process was at work in American life and at that time it seemed to me a good thing. So it also seemed to the Communist Party, but for a different reason. This professional leveling would fit teachers better into its class-struggle philosophy and so bring them to identify themselves with the proletariat.

At the convention were various interesting personalities: neat, quiet Albert Blumberg from Johns Hopkins University, the shrewdest communist agent in the Federation; Jerome Davis, just fired from the Yale Divinity School, thrown out, we were told, because he had dared promote a strike of student cafeteria workers; Mary Foley Grossman, president of the Philadelphia local, a fine and able woman; Miss Allie Mann, a good parliamentarian and charming woman from the largest Southern local of Atlanta, and one of the noncommunist leaders.

The convention was entirely swallowed up by the Communists. They passed every resolution they wanted and I began to feel that we had enough votes to pass a resolution for a Soviet America.

Jerome Davis was elected president of the Federation and his cause became the rallying point around which we fought during the next year. The fight for his reinstatement at Yale also became a Teachers Union cause.

The college division of the Federation voted to picket Yale and I was elected to a committee to negotiate with the Yale Corporation for his reinstatement. We were an unusual group of pickets for we wore caps and gowns and paraded with dignity on the beautiful campus, but we carried picket signs to show that we were the intellectual brothers of every worker on strike.

After some hours the Yale Corporation agreed to see a committee of three chosen from the delegation. I was one of them. In a gloomy paneled room with high ceilings we sat in high-backed chairs — my feet hardly touched the floor — and faced four members of the Corporation, silent men who would not talk except to say they were there only to listen. In vain we asked questions. The answer was always the same: they were there to listen, not to argue.

We outlined our demands. We made propaganda speeches about the role of American educators and about the right of a professor to participate in community problems. Then we reported to the assembled academic picketers that the power of concentrated wealth which the Yale Corporation represented had heard our remarks and promised to consider them.

As a result of our efforts the Corporation agreed to give Professor Davis a year's salary but refused to reinstate him. We were satisfied. He had got something out of our efforts and the Federation had a president who was a college professor.

The next convention was held in Madison, Wisconsin, the following year and again I was a delegate. Our Teachers Union had fared well that year in New York, having grown enormously in numbers, prestige, and victories. I had once again taken a leave of absence from Hunter in the spring of the year to represent the Union at the legislature. The trustees of the college had been reluctant to grant this leave but intercession by Mayor LaGuardia, with whom I was still on friendly terms, again assured my leave.

The CIO organization of mass unions and the rapid rise in union membership everywhere had brought great prestige and tremendous power to labor. We teachers rode on labor's coattails and were grateful to the Party for helping us to remain close to labor through all the shifts.

By 1937 the sit-down strikes in large plants and in WPA and welfare offices in New York fired the imagination of young intellectuals in the Teachers Union and we were eager to throw our lot in with the CIO. Wherever the Party teachers had influence we joined with strikers and walked in their picket lines. In New York we joined the newspapermen at the Brooklyn *Eagle* and at the Newark *Ledger;* at the telegraph offices we joined the communications workers. On the water front we gave time and money and even our homes to striking seamen. We marched in May Day parades in cap and gown.

That year we went to the convention hoping to take the Federation into John L. Lewis' CIO. We were fascinated by him, by his shaggy head and incredible eyebrows, by his biblical allusions, and by his Shakespearean acting. We were an odd group as I see it now, madcap intellectuals escaping from our classrooms, to teach workers' classes in Marxism and Leninism in our free hours. A few of the more astute paid only lip service to this activity, hoping to capture higher posts in academic circles where better service could be given to the cause. But most of the professors involved in this merry-go-round became better politicians than they were educators.

The convention at Madison had a large contingent of college professors, especially from teacher-training schools, and they began more and more to dominate the Federation. Among them were John de Boer and Dorothy Douglas and a score of brilliant left-wingers, including the attractive Hugh de Lacy from the West Coast. Even then De Lacy was engaged in splitting the Democratic Party by the formation of the Democratic Federation which resulted in his election to Congress. He was a valuable addition to the communist cause.

The Communist Party had told us that it did not want the teachers to go into the CIO. It felt it had enough power within the CIO whereas in the A.F. of L. the Party's forces were diminishing. I was bitterly disappointed for I believed that with the liberal CIO forces and its funds the Teachers Union movement could be vastly expanded. The A.F. of L. did not like to spend money in organizing teachers.

The Party took no chances on having its instructions miscarry. Rose Wortis and Roy Hudson, from the Central Committee, were at the convention hotel to steer the comrades aright. Roy was a tall, angular ex-seaman and Browder's labor specialist. He pounded the table and laid down the law. I told him frankly that I thought we ought to go with the CIO and Jerome Davis and the professors agreed. But we were informed that the Party did not wish it, and discipline was firm among the floor leaders. A vote was taken and we held to the Party line. The Communists uniting with some of the conservative members of the Federation defeated the CIO proposal.

In the city-wide 1937 elections in New York, the Party, which had helped establish the American Labor Party the year before, captured several important places within it. In city politics there was a steady elimination of differences between the major parties, and responsible leadership in the two old parties was disappearing. This led inevitably to the control of all parties by a small group around Fiorello LaGuardia, whose political heir was Vito Marcantonio. It was a personal dictatorship. Nominations were traded in the struggle for power, and the Communist Party was not slow in insinuating itself into this struggle.

Those who say LaGuardia was a great mayor forget that he did more to break down the major political parties and party responsibility than any other person in New York State. The streets were clean, taxes were lower, graft was less obvious, but under LaGuardia political power was transferred from the people organized into political parties into the hands of groups exercising personal power. The real political power passed to the well-financed, well-organized unions of the CIO and of the left-wing A.F. of L. and to the organized national minority groups, Negro, Italian, Jewish, etc. These groups were used as political machines to get votes and their self-appointed leaders were rewarded with the spoils of office. This new pattern I saw repeated over and over again, and it drained both Republican and Democratic Parties.

I saw LaGuardia meet with the Communists. I saw him accept from Si Gerson and Israel Amter written withdrawal from a position to which they had been nominated and receive a certificate of substitution at the mayor's request. A half-hour later I heard him address the Social Democrat wing of the American Labor Party at the Hotel Claridge, and the first thing he did was excoriate the Communists. Communists were in the audience and not one of

106

them seemed even to notice this humbug. Thus LaGuardia played with both wings of the Labor Party to his own advantage. Such were the politics to which the idealists were giving themselves.

The election campaign for 1937 was important to the left wing for it could begin now to make deals for power, with the Social Democrats of the American Labor Party, with the Democrats, with the Republicans, and with men of wealth who wanted public office and public spoils.

The American Labor Party that year supported the La-Guardia slate, which included Thomas Dewey for district attorney. I was surprised when Abe Unger, a Party lawyer whom I knew well, asked me to help organize a woman's committee for the election of Thomas Dewey. How Abe got into that campaign I do not know, but I do know that he organized for Dewey the labor groups which had earlier opposed him because of his investigations and prosecution of many unions.

I remember one especially hilarious Teachers Union meeting that year just before the election. It was held at the Hotel Diplomat and we were cheering the candidates of the American Labor Party and its allies when Thomas Dewey, accompanied by his campaign managers, whizzed into the meeting and whizzed out again after making a short speech. And I thought, with satirical amusement, that politics does indeed make strange bedfellows.

By 1938 my work for the Union and for the schools was engaging me so deeply that it interfered with my work as a teacher, so I decided to resign from Hunter and take a full-time position with the Union.

Many of my friends were surprised to hear of my decision. They were amazed that I should be willing to leave the college, my tenure, and my pension, and other rights

107

for an uncertain union job at a reduced salary, and worst of all for a job dependent on yearly elections.

President Colligan was deeply distressed when I told him and he asked me to reconsider. "These people will take you and use you, Bella," he warned me, "and then they will throw you away."

I looked at him. I could see that he was sincerely troubled about me and I appreciated it. But I thought him old-fashioned and fearful of new viewpoints. Besides, I knew he was a Catholic and opposed to the forces with which I was associated.

I shook my head. "No, I have decided," I told him. "In this country one hundred and forty million Americans have no tenure and no security. I'll take my chances with them." And I handed him my resignation from Hunter College.

CHAPTER NINE

I GAVE UP my Hunter College work mainly because I felt I could not serve two masters. If I remained a teacher, I felt my undivided attention ought to be given to my students and not shared with outside organizations. I was afraid also that, if I remained a teacher, as many teacher politicians did, there would be a conflict between my desire to serve the interests of the college and my sense of dedication to the interests of the "downtrodden."

I made the choice without regard for the future, confident that in the working class I should find satisfaction and security. As the legislative year again approached, I became a full-time employee of the Teachers Union at sixty dollars a week. This is the salary I received during the years I worked for the Union. I did not then or later ask for an increase. I was sensitive about workers' money. I had heard so much about "pie card artists" who were the opportunists and careerists in the trade-unions movement that I did not want to tempt myself. I worked for the Union for eight years at that salary.

In that first year I devoted myself especially to pressuring the New York Board of Education to fulfill its moral obligation to thousands of substitute teachers who had been in the schools during the depression as per-diem employees. They taught a full program on a par with the regularly appointed teachers in all things except that they did not receive an annual wage, had no vacation pay, and were docked for every day ill or absent. These teachers hated holidays, for on those days they went unpaid, and they had no pension rights. They were called "substitute" teachers, but they were not substituting for anyone.

The result was an educational jungle in which only the most strident voices could be heard. In fact the law of the jungle itself was sometimes followed. The WPA teachers, the substitutes, the instructors' associations in the colleges, were goaded by a sense of injustice and a fear of failure. This was the lush soil in which the communist teachers' fraction in the Teachers Union flourished.

The fact that the opportunity for free public education was provided in New York City from grades through college without expense to parents, with even textbooks free, created an intellectual proletariat. These men and women needed jobs commensurate with their education, and teaching at that time was the work most sought by them. When these would-be teachers began to run into the political ineptness and the callous do-nothing policy of the educational authorities there was bound to be conflict.

In the substitute teachers' campaign I attracted thousands of nonunion teachers. I felt I had to find a way to help them. And in a quiet way they began to be grateful to the Communists.

There were dark by-products of the struggle. The younger teachers who had been forced into the WPA and substitute-teacher categories were the children of the most recent immigrants, the Italians, the Greeks, the Jews from Russia, and the Slavs. Merging with this group were the children of the expanding Negro population of the city who were qualified educationally for professional jobs. The positions of power and of educational supervision, however, were held mostly by persons of English, Scotch, and Irish origin.

The Communists, who are unerring in attaching themselves to an explosive situation, had their answers for these troubled young teachers. Their chief answer was that we had reached the "breakdown of the capitalist system." To those who were self-conscious on race or religion they said that "religious or racial discrimination" was the cause. When individual instances of bigotry and discrimination arose, the Communists were quick to note them and to exaggerate them. So a cleavage was established between the older teachers, who were largely Protestants, Catholics, and conservative Jews, and the new teachers who were increasingly freethinkers, atheists, or agnostics, and sometimes called themselves "humanists."

The Teachers Union was in a dilemma on the substitute teacher question. On the one hand, it wanted to cater to the older and more established teachers who were saying that the Union was championing only the rag, tag, and bobtail of the profession. On the other hand, it knew that the substitutes of today would be the regulars of the future, and besides more Communists could be recruited from those pinched economically.

The fraction leaders of the Union were divided on the issue. Some were willing to drop it because they wanted to hold a position of authority among the regular teachers, so that they could influence educational policy and curriculum change. I sometimes came back from Albany to find the old guard with set, grim faces, and I knew they had been discussing the disavowal of the campaign for the substitute teachers.

To me it was a cause, and I appealed to the Party for a decision. I received a favorable one.

I now began consciously to build new Party leadership in the Union. I surrounded myself with younger Party members who were more alert to new situations and did not think in rigid Marxist patterns.

We did not succeed in passing the substitute-teacher legislation for which we fought at Albany. But we made it the most controversial legislation of the 1938 sessions. Later, when it was passed by the legislature, Governor Lehman vetoed it reluctantly after the entire Board of Education had used its power against it. However, in vetoing it he urged New York City to do something about the situation. He added that if the city failed to do so he would act favorably on such legislation in the future.

The Union and the communist group grew immeasurably in stature and prestige among the new crop of teachers and among other civil-service employees. Even politicians and public officials respected us for our relentless campaign.

I was weary at the end of that session. Yet I stayed in Albany to attend the State Constitutional Convention, determined to write into the new constitution guarantees for an expanding public-school system. Charles Poletti, former lieutenant governor and Supreme Court judge, was secretary of the Convention, and he, together with Edward Weinfeld, now a federal judge, was helpful in safeguarding the achievements of the public-school system.

In the fall of 1938, the American Labor Party nominated me for the Assembly in the old Tenth Assembly district, the area including Greenwich Village. It was a famous district represented at various times by Herbert Brownell and MacNeil Mitchell. On the ticket with me and running for Congress from the same area was George Backer, at that time married to Dorothy Schiff, owner of the *New York Post*. It was the period when the Alex Rose-David Dubinsky wing of the Labor Party and the communist wing were still in coalition — an uneasy alliance born of expediency. Both were seeking control of New York State politics.

The Teachers Union organized my campaign committee. We wrote political songs, made recordings, and did a great deal of street-corner speaking. By this time I had taken part in so many election campaigns in difficult areas that I developed a facility for speechmaking. One of my favorite charges was that the candidates of the Republican Party and of the Democratic Party were lawyers connected with the same law partnership, a firm which represented the public-utility interests. We used to enlarge on this fact, and concluded with "Tweedledum and Tweedledee — you'd better vote the ALP."

Late one evening, as I was winding up a street-corner meeting at Seventh Avenue and Fourteenth Street, I saw David Dubinsky, who lived in the neighborhood, and George Meany go by. They stopped to listen for a few moments, then smiled at each other, and went on. Suddenly, and for the first time, there came over me a sense of futility over this endless activity in which the Communists were involving me.

That year John and I were living in a small and charming house on West Eleventh Street. My parents occupied one floor, John and I the next, and the duplex above us we rented to Susan Woodruff and her husband. Susan was a dear old lady whose husband was a Princeton graduate and a Republican. Susan, on the other hand, was an avowed Communist and admirer of the Soviet Union, though like her husband she traced her ancestry to the early settlers of America. Later she became one of the three old ladies who ostensibly owned the *Daily Worker*.

I loved Susan and respected her for the honesty of her open affection for the Soviet Union. She had gone to Russia in the thirties and had taken pictures of Soviet scenes. These she had arranged in slides and she offered to show them free as well as give a lecture to churches and Y's. She genuinely believed that the Soviet Union meant an advance for humanity and she was eager to do her part in strengthening it.

The Party was always happy to use such voluntary propagandists. Even anti-communists never attempted to show such people as Susan that Communists and their fellow travelers were helping to undermine not a selfish capitalist class, but the very life of her own group. She was surrounded by like-minded people, Mary van Kleek of the Russell Sage Foundation, Josephine Truslow Adams, Annie Pennypacker, and Ferdinanda Reed. When I saw Susan and others of old American families devoted to the principles of service to humanity it helped to allay any doubts I had.

At the end of 1938 we gave up our house in the Village and moved to one in Poughkeepsie because my parents wanted to be in the country. My father's health was failing. My mother welcomed the chance to be in the country again. I kept a room in the city and went home for week ends. John was often away on business and the rest of the time he stayed in Poughkeepsie, for he, too, preferred country living.

The legislative session of 1939 had reflected the now-deepening depression which had been gathering momentum. The public hearings on the state budget which took place on Lincoln's Birthday brought demands for a cut

114

in state aid to education. It was a struggle now between the organized taxpayer group with the slogan, "Ax the tax," and the Teachers Union which led an army of teachers and parents with the counter slogan, "Don't use the ax on the child." But a ten per cent cut in state aid was passed — a cut which we felt endangered the education program and meant a loss of teachers' jobs.

At the end of the session the legislature passed a resolution calling for a legislative investigation into the costs of education and of the administrative procedures of education. There was a rider at the end calling for an investigation into the subversive activities of teachers in New York City.

I called immediate attention to the fact that the study of the costs of education was tied to one for investigating subversive activities. I concluded that the legislative leaders wanted to reduce costs, but that in order to do so it would be necessary to smear the teachers. I charged they were using a Red-baiting technique to undermine education.

Neither Mayor LaGuardia nor the officials of the American Labor Party would move to ward off this attack. A legislative committee was appointed, headed by Senator Frederic Coudert, a Republican from New York City, and Herbert Rapp, a Republican from upstate. Other teacher organizations discounted this attack on the educational budget and regarded it merely as an attack on the Teachers Union, and no doubt were secretly pleased.

In April 1939 John called me in Albany and urged me to come home immediately. My father was dying in St. Francis Hospital in Poughkeepsie.

I was very grateful to John that despite his hostility to Catholicism he had recognized my father's wishes and had

115

called a Catholic doctor and then taken him to a Catholic hospital. Ruth Jenkins, my secretary, drove me at a furious speed through a night of sleety rain. When I reached the hospital, my father was alone behind screens with an oxygen tank beside him, unconscious or asleep.

A nun attending him told me he had received the last rites. I felt thankful though I had long since ceased believing in such things myself. I did feel that something was needed to lessen the pain of dying and to give life meaning.

As I stood by my father's bedside looking at him, my hand over his, he opened his eyes, still so blue and bright, and, though he could not speak, he looked at me steadily, and then a single tear fell from his eye. It cut into me and troubled me for years afterward, for somehow it seemed to represent his sorrow about me. I thought, with remorse, how in these cluttered years I had failed him as a daughter and had left him without my companionship.

He was buried in St. Peter's Cemetery at Poughkeepsie. There were not many at the funeral but the town officials gave him a motor escort to the cemetery, as evidence of their affection for him as a friend and good citizen. After the funeral I went back to Albany with a heavy heart to face a mass of work.

The Communist Party had been quick to realize that to avert the attack on the communist teachers, a thing which might lead to the heart of the Party, it must help the campaign against the pending Rapp-Coudert investigation. In a move to spare the Union the strain of all this and also to bring people other than teachers into the fight, we organized a committee called "Friends of the Free Public Schools." Under its aegis we collected funds, more than $150,000 the first year. We published attractive booklets which we sent to teacher organizations, to trade unions, to women's clubs, to public officials.

I set up a booth and an exhibit at the New York State Fair in Syracuse and I covered numerous county fairs, issuing a strident call for aid to the public schools. We got free time on dozens of radio programs. We put on interesting programs over a radio station in New York. We organized "Save Our Schools" community clubs, made up of teachers, parents, trade unionists, students, and young people. We were a well-trained army and by our well-organized action we gave people a feeling that in the long run we would win.

That summer saw a new attack on the New York Teachers Union. Friends of Dr. Lefkowitz, largely from the professorial group in the American Federation of Teachers, together with a socialist bloc, some old-line A.F. of L. members, and some anti-communists, were organized. They were under leadership of Dr. George Counts and Professor John Childs of Teachers College, Professor George Axtelle of Chicago, the socialist teachers' bloc of Detroit, the Teachers Union of Atlanta, Selma Borchard of Washington, and George Googe who was the A.F. of L. representative at the convention that year. These, together with New York City minority groups, chief among whom were Lovestonites led by Ben Davidson (later secretary of the Liberal Party of New York City) and his wife Eve, formed a mixed group but it united for one objective.

They planned to take the leadership in the Federation from the Communists. But the Party brought in reserve strength from the Northwest, from California, from the South, in addition to its forces in the East and New England. We had not been too successful in the Middle West, where the conservative Chicago Teachers Union and the

St. Paul and Minneapolis teachers with their large locals swamped the small locals of college teachers and private schoolteachers which we had been able to establish. Loss of control faced the Communists.

To make matters worse, news of the Soviet-Nazi pact broke during the week of the convention, with the result that we were now driven into a minority position. Even though some hidden Communists remained in office, we were powerless to use the American Federation of Teachers to help the distraught New York locals. We feared that the newly elected officers would do their own investigating of the New York situation, and perhaps lift our charters.

The Soviet-Nazi collaboration came at a time when the civilized world could no longer remain silent at the Nazi atrocities against Jews and other minorities. The large Jewish membership of the unions under the leadership of David Dubinsky and Alex Rose had its own reasons for hating the Communists, reasons arising out of the old feuds and the struggle to control unions, and because of the untrustworthiness of the Communists in joint enterprises. Now these people were genuinely outraged at the picture of Molotov shaking hands with Von Ribbentrop.

The Jewish people within the Party were also disturbed and quite a few left it. Those who remained, rationalized the event on the ground that the warmongers of the West wanted to destroy the Soviet Fatherland, so in self-defense it had outfoxed the Western "warmongers" by making an alliance with their enemy. I was too busy with the teachers' problem to give much attention to this outrage though it troubled me.

Though the Communists supported Mayor LaGuardia in the election campaigns I became impatient with his attitude on teacher problems and finally to exert pressure we threw a picket line around City Hall. We made a singing picket line; twenty-four hours of it, an all-day and all-night picketing and, as a publicity stunt, I announced to the press that there would be prayers at sunrise. I tried to get a Catholic priest to say the sunrise prayers for us, but even the priests from the poor parishes around City Hall looked at me oddly and said they could not do it without permission from the chancery. I offered to pay them, to make a contribution to their charities, but they only eyed me more oddly and refused with thanks. Eventually a liberal minister agreed to come and lead our pickets in prayer.

The Party did not arrange for that picket line but it was pleased when the news hit the front pages of the newspapers and they used pictures of the pickets at morning prayer. Strange as it may seem, I believe we did pray that morning.

This episode ended my friendship with LaGuardia, for he was furious at the adverse publicity. It did accomplish something. The Board of Education was ordered to look into the situation of the substitute teachers.

By fall of 1939 the Rapp-Coudert Committee had settled down to work with a score of investigators. On the committee were men I could not dislike, mild, fair men such as Robert Morris, Philip Haberman of the Anti-Defamation League, and Charles S. Whitman, son of the former governor of New York.

Assemblyman Rapp was an up-stater concerned chiefly with educational finance and administration. So he played a negligible role in the investigation.

That left one person on whom to turn our combined fury. Senator Coudert was a Republican, cold and patrician in appearance. Because of his international law firm with an office in Paris and the fact that it acted for many White

Russians, we looked on him as an agent of imperialism. From the Communist Party and from the men who represented the Soviet interests in this country we got the go-ahead signal to make him our target. The Party placed its forces at the teachers' disposal, since the teachers were now in the vanguard holding the line in defense of the Party itself.

I knew that the fight would be bitter, but I was not prepared for its violence. The first attack was on the membership lists of the Teachers Union. Within the Union there were still those who belonged to the splinter groups, Lovestonites, Trotskyites, Socialists, but in the course of the fight in 1940 these splinter groups left the Union and busied themselves in other organizations. Local Five was served with a demand, a subpoena *duces tecum,* by the Rapp-Coudert Committee to produce all our records, membership lists, and financial reports.

There was general consultation. The Party established a joint chief-of-staff group with several from the teachers' fraction. It included such Party leaders as Israel Amter, Jack Stackel, Charles Krumbein, all from Party headquarters, and several of the Party's lawyers. They were a top command to direct operations. The strategy decided on was to defend the teachers by defending the Party. The lesser policy, or tactics, was to be established from day to day.

For the "Committee to Defend the Public Schools" we hired a battery of lawyers, as it was impossible for one lawyer to attend to the many demands. We decided to fight the seizure of our Union membership lists all the way to the Court of Appeals. This would gain time and enable us to continue organizing the mass campaigns against the legislative committee. It would also serve to wear out the investigating committee.

120

To protect our membership lists we appealed for trade-union support. We sent speakers to union meetings on the water front, to the hotel and restaurant workers, to the meat cutters, to the state, county, and municipal workers, both A.F. of L. and CIO. We trained speakers, prepared speakers' outlines, mimeographed form resolutions, and sent hundreds of form telegraph messages to the governor and to majority and minority leaders.

We tried even the impossible. I remember one state A.F. of L. meeting in Albany presided over by Tom Lyons, then its president. I asked for the floor, made an appeal for support, reminded the delegates that the struggle for union organization had been a long and tough one, that at one time union men carried their cards in the soles of their shoes. I pointed out that though it was our Union which was under attack, it might be theirs tomorrow. Then I moved for support.

I got none whatsoever. The communist delegates in that audience were afraid to speak up. And then I saw that there was more compassion in the face of Tom Lyons who was opposed to everything I stood for than in the faces of the comrades who were preserving their own skins.

It had been our decision that membership lists were not to be turned over to the Committee even if we lost in the courts. The membership files were turned over to me and I was ordered to refuse to turn the lists in, preferring jail if necessary. I happened to be out of the office when the Committee came to demand them, and Miss Wallas, in whose custody were the public schoolteacher lists, gave them to the representatives of the Committee, presumably at Mr. Hendley's direction.

I burned the lists of the college Union teachers which were in my possession. We were afraid that through them the Committee would be able to trace a pattern of membership, since our cards showed who sponsored each individual and the date on which he joined.

Once the Committee got the cards it began to issue subpoenas. We instructed those teachers who were not Party members to appear before the Committee and to tell the truth. But there were hundreds for whom the truth might mean dismissal, and these we decided to protect.

The Party now placed at our services its intelligence apparatus, for the Communist Party has its own intelligence officers, in splinter groups, in the trade unions, in major divisions of our body politic, in the police departments, and in intelligence divisions of the Government. I was to see some proof of its efficiency. For no sooner did the Rapp-Coudert Committee begin to issue subpoenas than I got a message from Chester, who was in charge of the Party Intelligence, assuring me he had arranged for a liaison who would meet me regularly with information on what was going on in the Rapp-Coudert Committee.

I met my contact daily, in cafeterias, restaurants, and public buildings. She was an attractive, aristocratic blonde, well-dressed and charming. She gave me slips of paper which bore the names of those witnesses whom the Committee was using to get information and a list of those who were to be subpoenaed.

Armed with this advance information, we would go to the Union members who were to be called and warn them. If we wanted to gain time, the person was told to send word he was sick, even enter a hospital if necessary. If it were feasible, he was to move. If not, we assigned a lawyer or a Union representative to go with the person to the hearing. Most of the teachers were instructed not to answer questions and to take a possible contempt citation. Some were instructed to resign from their jobs, because

122

we feared the Committee would publish the facts about their international connections. If the teachers told the truth, they might involve other Party contacts.

The Coudert Committee issued more than six hundred subpoenas. The teachers over whom the Party had control followed our directions and instructions. Because they were forewarned by us they were able, with our assistance, to prepare defense stories to give the Committee. After each person had been down to the Committee meeting he was instructed by us to write an exact résumé of what had transpired with all the questions and answers, and these were delivered to our Defense Committee. We studied these résumés for possible evidence of the trend of the Committee's inquiry so that we could better arm the next batch of teachers to be called.

It was while I was going over these stories that I realized for the first time just how important a part of the communist movement in America the teachers were. They touched practically every phase of Party work. They were not used only as teachers in Party education, where they gave their services free of charge, but in the summer they traveled and visited Party figures in other countries. Most of them were an idealistic, selfless lot who manned front committees and were the backbone of the Party's strength in the Labor Party and later in the Progressive Party. Even in the inner Party apparatus they performed invaluable services. They provided the Party with thousands of contacts among young people, women's organizations, and professional groups. They were generous in helping finance Party activities. Some supported husbands who were Party organizers or on special assignment for the Party.

There is no doubt that the Rapp-Coudert investigation of New York City schools provided the legislature with a great deal of information on how Communists work. It also provided a good example of how they fight back, sometimes by a defensive fight against those conducting the investigation and with every weapon at the Party's disposal, including smearing, name-calling, frameup, careful combing of each investigator's history and background. If there is nothing that can be attacked, then some innuendo is whispered which by repetition snowballs into a smear and makes the public say, "Where there is smoke there must be fire."

Sometimes the campaign is on the offensive. Some angle is found to explain the evil motives of those who are conducting the investigation, perhaps to show that the investigation is itself a blind for some ulterior motive and that the result will deprive people of certain rights. In the teacher fight we steadfastly kept before the public the idea that the investigation was intended to rob the public schools of financial support and to promote religious and racial bigotry.

Little by little we won the campaign, at least in the opinion of many people; and we distracted the attention of the public from the specific work of the Committee. Support for the teachers, which at first had come only from the Communist Party, increased and included liberals, left trade unions, national group organizations, religious organizations, then political parties of the left, then left-wing Democrats, then so-called Progressive Republicans. All the support, however, was for tangential issues and not the basic issue. It did not matter to us so long as they marched at our side. Their reasons were unimportant to us.

The United States was in process of being coaxed into an alliance with England and France at this time. At first the Communist Party was in seeming opposition to this because of the Soviet-Nazi pact, and United Party members became anti-war. Party groups began making alliances with the most vicious pro-Hitler groups in America. These communist activities of a low order always suck in those who begin as more or less sincere but misguided idealists but remain to follow the Party blindly. The *Daily Worker* editorials continuously blasted the Rapp-Coudert Committee as a technique of the warmongers.

The American Communists came close to pacifism in those days. This phase did not last, but in the course of it the Teachers Defense Committee published a book called *Winter Soldiers*, of which some ten thousand copies were printed. It was beautifully illustrated. We had cartoons contributed by leading artists because the proceeds were to go to the Defense Committee. But we were forced to desist from further distribution when we learned that the International Communist line had changed once again and the Party was now pro-war, as the Communist International had always intended that America should be.

The International had frightened the Western world by its alliance with Hitler; now the campaign to involve America in the world war was once again in full swing. This time the Party had some difficulty, because so many new friends of the Party found it difficult to swing nonchalantly from a support of pacifism to a support of war. Thousands of students under the impetus of the Communists had taken the Oxford oath against war. Many had read with joy the anti-war poems of Mike Quinn, who had also provided the CIO with its slogan, "The Yanks are not coming." Thousands of women had worked with the Party on its mass committees, such as the League against War and Fascism — a title which was later changed to American Committee for Peace and Democracy, and then to American Mobilization Committee.

In 1940 I had been selected by the Party to lead a committee called Women's Trade Union Committee for Peace. We raised money, hired a young man to do public relations, and arranged a mass delegation to Washington. There we lobbied with representatives and senators. We went on the air with pro-German speakers. We set up a continuous picket line in front of the White House.

It had been at this time that a final break came between my husband and myself. For some time John had been disturbed by my increasing activity with the Communists. He himself was pro-British. He had served in the Canadian Air Service during World War I until America's entry. He despised what he called the "phony peace" campaigns. There were other and personal reasons why our marriage had not been successful, but the breaking point came at this time. He told me he was leaving for Florida to get a divorce.

I stayed on at our apartment in Perry Street. My mother had come to live with us some months before. I shuttled back and forth between Albany and New York that spring, devoting all my time to the Union and other Party causes. It was during these months that I developed my deepest loyalty to the Communist Party. In great part this was because I was grateful to them for their support of the teachers.

I still did not see communism as a conspiracy. I regarded it as a philosophy of life which glorified the "little people." I was surrounded by people who called themselves Communists and who were warmhearted people like myself. In the world outside there was immorality and decadence and injustice; there was no real standard to live by. But among the Communists I knew there was moral behavior according to well-defined standards and there was a semblance of order and certitude.

126

The rest of the world had become cold and chaotic to me. I heard talk of brotherhood, but I saw no evidence of it. In the group of Communists with which I worked I did find a community of interest.

In addition to the Teachers Union work I continued as an active leader of the American Labor Party. I was assigned to work with a committee to free the leaders of the Furriers Union who had been sent to prison for industrial sabotage. I organized a committee of women, including the wives of the imprisoned men, to visit congressmen and the Department of Justice.

We talked with Mrs. Eleanor Roosevelt at her apartment on Eleventh Street. She graciously agreed to do all in her power to get our memoranda into the hands of the appropriate officials. She was sympathetic with the wives of the imprisoned men who had come with me.

Only one note in the interview disturbed me. The matter of the right of Communists to be leaders of trade unions had come up in the general discussion. Mrs. Roosevelt said that she believed Communists should be permitted to be members but not leaders of trade unions.

The position seemed illogical to me and I said so. Communism cannot be right for little people, for the workers, and wrong for the leaders. There can be only one moral code for all. Perhaps Mrs. Roosevelt, like myself and many other well-meaning people in America, has by this time learned that there is no halfway house in which you can meet the communist movement. Co-existence is not possible on any level.

In the summer of 1940 we attended the American Federation of Teachers convention in Buffalo, fearful of our welcome. It was almost ironic that once again we were at a convention at a time when the international communist scene was stirred by a dramatic event. The previous year we had heard of the signing of the Soviet-Nazi pact; now came news of the murder of Leon Trotsky in Mexico. The combined Socialists, Trotskyites, and Lovestone group practically held us responsible for this event. But the real result of that 1940 convention was the fact that the George Counts group took control of the American Federation of Teachers and soon after the New York, Philadelphia, and other communist-led locals had their charters lifted. In New York the coveted charter of the American Federation of Teachers affiliation went to Dr. Lefkowitz and the new organization he had built, the Teachers Guild.

This automatically ended our formal relations with the A.F. of L. The New York Teachers Union was now an independent union not affiliated with either of the great labor movements. I thought bitterly of that convention in Madison when we would have been welcomed into the CIO, but the Party forbade it. The loss of the charter had come about chiefly as a result of the unfavorable publicity given us during the Rapp-Coudert investigation and by foreign events.

I returned to New York to learn more bad news. Nearly fifty of our teachers had been suspended from their jobs. But perhaps the greatest blow was the indictment of one of our teachers, Morris U. Schappes, on the charge of perjury. An English teacher at City College, an ardent Communist, himself a graduate of City College, he was the child of parents who lived close to want on the lower East Side. With his devoted wife, Sonia, he lived as dedicated a life, that is, as dedicated to communism, as anyone I ever met. He was the flame that fired the City College boys, and the teachers, too, when their revolutionary devotion ebbed. Under the name of "Horton" he was the New York Party director of education while he was still teaching at City College. He had exercised tremendous influence on class after class in the college, and in the organizing of the college teachers into the Union he had worked indefatigably.

When he was subpoenaed by the Committee, it was decided that he should either refuse to answer certain questions and take a contempt citation with almost certain loss of his job, or resign from it. When I returned from Albany, I learned that the top-level committee in my absence had again changed the decision: he was to admit he was a Communist and say that he and three others published the Communist shop paper, the *Pen and Hammer*, which was circulated anonymously at City College.

The trouble was that the three Communists he named were either dead or gone from the college and the Coudert Committee was able to prove that his statement was a falsehood. Morris Schappes was indicted and brought to trial before Judge Jonah Goldstein, remanded to the old Tombs, with bail set at ten thousand dollars.

When the doors of the dirty old rat-infested Tombs closed on him I hated the world I lived in. It didn't seem possible that ordinary men could put a man in jail when his only desire was to improve the condition of the poor, when he gained nothing personally from his activities. I hated Tom Dewey, the district attorney, whom I blamed for the catastrophe. I hated the "system" which I thought was at the bottom of the tragedy. I went to Sonia and did what I could to help her.

We organized a committee for Schappes' defense. We held a mass meeting in front of the New York Supreme Court in Foley Square and laid a wreath on the steps of the courthouse "in memory of academic freedom." For this was the issue we injected into the Schappes case to gain public support. Meantime, I received ten thousand dollars in cash from one of the Party's friends and Morris was out of jail pending appeals.

About this case there is still a certain irony. Schappes' trial attorney, Edmund Kuntz, was one of the trial lawyers in the Rosenberg atom spy case. It is equally ironical that Morris Schappes was one of the teachers who inspired Julius Rosenberg at City College while he was a student there.

At the end of the trial Morris Schappes was convicted and sentenced to two to four years in State Prison.

A new period was at hand, a period of extremes, when the united front of Communists and the forces of national unity in the United States were to work together to win the war. Morris Schappes was forgotten except by his wife and a few loyal friends. The Communist Party was now in coalition with the forces which had prosecuted Morris.

Late 1940 and early 1941 had been spent in endless preparation of the defenses of individuals who were brought up before the school boards for dismissals based on the Rapp-Coudert Committee findings. When the smoke cleared, we found there had been a loss of from forty to fifty positions in the city colleges and in the public schools. The Teachers Union had, by and large, withstood the attack. Some loss of membership took place but we still had close to one thousand Party members in a union of about four thousand.

In February of 1941 my dearly loved mother was taken ill. The diagnosis was pneumonia. I was in Albany when word came. I hurried back to find to my distress that agents of the Rapp-Coudert Committee and overzealous newspaper reporters had broken into my apartment in search of teachers' lists. My mother, in her broken English, had informed them that I was away and would be glad to see them when I returned. She refused to let them look at any of my papers but they had pushed her aside and tried to take over. I was furious when I learned of this illegal invasion of my home. But everyone disclaimed responsibility and my chief concern at the moment was my mother.

She was seventy-six years old. She had always been strong in body and she had continued to have the lively mind of her earlier days. I had never seen her bored. Her one worry was that I worked too hard, and she often pleaded with me to relax, but I was driven by inner furies. I took no rest. I did not take vacations. I liked to say there was no vacation from the class struggle.

For a long time my activities had no meaning to my mother. All she knew was that I worked too hard. But she must have known something in her later days, for once she shook her head and looked at me sadly and said, "America does strange things to children."

She died in my arms one night several weeks later. In the repose of death her face was lovely, and as I stood by her body I suddenly saw my mother in her big white sweater with loaves of bread in her hands, striding across the fields at Pilgrim's Rest. All around her were the wild birds who knew she had come to feed them. She helped birds and animals and children and grownups. I would miss her greatly.

Services for her were held at the Church of Our Lady of Pompeii on Bleecker Street. There were not many people in the church with me, but Beatrice came and some of the Party teachers were there, people alien to this house of God. They came to comfort my loss. I was deeply touched.

My mother was buried in St. Peter's Cemetery in Pough-keepsie beside my father and I came back to New York. Now I was entirely alone. My personal life seemed completely at an end and I belonged only to the cause I served.

I moved out of the apartment because I could not bear

its loneliness. I found a tiny, inexpensive one on Horatio Street on the top floor of an old house near the Hudson River. There was a window beside my bed and from it I could see the morning sky when I woke up.

Sometimes I thought, as I lay there, how long a way I had come to loneliness. How far behind me was the room in the embrace of the horsechestnut tree in the house with my mother and my father and the children of our family, and where I had planned my future.

I still had a room and I still had a family. The room was far different from the one at Pilgrim's Rest and my family was a great, impersonal family. In its midst I could find forgetfulness when my body was completely spent and my brain was weary.

CHAPTER TEN

I T WAS THE SUMMER OF 1941. The Teachers Union hoped that the American Federation of Teachers at its convention would grant readmission to our local. We therefore elected a full delegation and sent it to Detroit, the convention city. But those who now controlled the American Federation of Teachers were hardly aware of any change in the situation. Having expelled the Communists the previous year, they were not ready to sit down to a peaceful convention with them this year. They refused to seat the delegates of the expelled locals.

We held a rival convention across the street. We made speeches, and many delegates from the regular convention came to listen to us. But we returned to New York without having realized our objective.

On the way back to New York, a number of delegates, including Dale Zysman and myself, were in the same train with Dr. Counts and Professor Childs, top men of the American Federation of Teachers. Dale, always an excellent mixer, went over to sit down with them and talked of possible future readmission. Both professors thought it proper that the United States should become an ally of the USSR but they felt that the American Communist Party should be disbanded. This was a political philosophy I did not understand at the time. Later that year the same two men published a book entitled *America, Russia and the Communist Party in the Post-War World,* a fulsome eulogy of the Soviet Union with an appeal for co-operation in war and in peace between the United States and the USSR. But they called for disbanding of the Communist Party.

That fall I was still trying to find jobs for teachers who had lost their positions in the Rapp-Coudert fight. A number of those suspended were still awaiting departmental trials. The Party was no longer interested in them. Its new line was a united front with all the "democratic forces" — meaning all the pro-war forces.

Before June 1941 it had been an "imperialist war" for the redivision of markets, a war which could have only reactionary results. But when the Soviet Union was attacked, the war was transformed into a "people's war," a "war of liberation."

The American Communist Party dropped all its campaigns of opposition. Its pacifist friends were again "Fascist reactionaries" and all its energy was employed in praise of France and England as great democracies. The fight against the Board of Higher Education had to be brought to an end because the Party regarded Mayor LaGuardia as a force in the pro-democratic war camp.

Through an intermediary we offered to make a wholesale deal on the balance of cases remaining untried before the Board of Higher Education. We were unsuccessful and had to deal with the cases one by one.

In the legislative program of the Teachers Union for

1941 I included a proposal to establish public nursery schools. The WPA nursery-school program which had been under the State Department of Education was coming to an end. The bill I introduced for the Union was mild. It was conceived mainly as a program of jobs for teachers and partly as a social program to aid working women with small children. The storm of opposition from conservative groups startled me. Evidently I had stumbled on a controversial issue, one which struck at the role of the mother in education.

I, myself, had given educational policy scant attention. Little that was controversial had been included in my education courses at Hunter College, and in my graduate work I had steered clear of such courses, feeling that my main emphasis must be on subject matter. I held to an old-fashioned theory that if a teacher knew her subject, and had a few courses in psychology and liked young people, she should be able to teach. I had been horrified to see teachers, who were going to teach mathematics or history or English, spend all the time of their graduate work in courses on methods of teaching.

On December 7, 1941, I called together a few outstanding citizens to discuss the program of school expansion and to solicit support for nursery schools and better adult education. The meeting was held at the home of Mrs. Elinor Gimbel, a public-spirited woman, interested in many causes.

With us was Stanley Isaacs, liberal Republican from Manhattan's silk-stocking district, which was headed by Senator Coudert. Also present was Judge Anna Kross, Commissioner of Correction in New York City; Kenneth Leslie, former editor of the magazine *The Protestant;* and Elizabeth Hawes, fashionable dressmaker and author of *Fashion Is Spinach.*

We had enjoyed Mrs. Gimbel's hospitality and talked

about discrimination, about the new waves of population in New York, about the conflict with Catholics on federal aid, about budgets, school buildings, and teachers' salaries.

As I look back over the conferences I attended on educational policies and methods and progress, I realize that we never discussed or thought about what kind of man or woman we expected to develop by our educational system. What were the goals of education? How were we to achieve them? These questions few asked. Are we asking them today in the higher echelons of the public schools, and what are our conclusions?

Only recently I heard the chief of the New York public schools speak on television on juvenile delinquency. It was soon after the wrecking of a school by young vandals. He said that what was needed was more buildings, more teachers, better playgrounds. Those devoted to progressive education and to preparing youth to live in the "new socialist world" are abstractly sure of what they want, but they seem not to know that they work with human beings. Aside from teaching that children must learn to get along with other children, no moral or natural law standards are set. There is no word about how our children are to find the right order of harmonious living.

I, too, had to learn by hard experience that you cannot cure a sick soul with more buildings or more playgrounds. These are important, but they are not enough. Abraham Lincoln, schooled in a one-room log cabin, received from education what all the athletic fields and laboratories cannot give. All his speeches reflected his love for his Creator. He knew that God is the cure for godlessness.

On this Sunday afternoon of December 7, 1941, we talked long and ardently on education. We talked, too, of the splendid work done by the women of England for the safety of their children in preparation for bombing attacks. Mrs. Gimbel finally turned on the radio to give us the news. And as the first sounds came we heard an excited voice announcing that Pearl Harbor had been bombed by Japanese planes. The distant calamity in Europe which we had been discussing in this pleasant room was now ours. We listened appalled as the voice told us the full horror of what had happened.

When the news announcement was over, we looked at each other in silence for a few minutes. We were people of many races and religions and parties, but we were of one mind on America. So it was only natural that we immediately set to work to make plans, and that these plans dealt with children. Then and there we formed ourselves into an emergency Child Care Committee with Mrs. Gimbel as chairman, and to this committee I promised to turn over my files on nursery schools and to give all my assistance.

In the Party we had long expected that the war would involve the United States. In fact, earlier in the summer the Party had ominously turned its Committee on Peace into the American Mobilization Committee (for war), and in September we had held a huge outdoor meeting at the Brooklyn Velodrome. I was one of the speakers. The keynote of the meeting was the coming war and how to meet it.

The energies of the Party were now turned to establishing win-the-war committees. The old feuds of the Teachers Union and the CIO and the A.F. of L. were put into moth balls and the little arguments and the big ones were forgotten. Now the Communists became peacemakers between discordant factions everywhere. With joy and relief I watched the Party serve as an agency for drawing the forces of the community together to win the war.

Of course the Communist Party was overjoyed at what

was happening. It moved briskly to place the colossal strength of America at the disposal of the Soviet Union. Moreover, the rank-and-file Communists were once again tasting the joy of being accepted by all groups. The Party line made it possible during this period for ordinary Party members to be merely human beings and to act naturally, for their neighbors were now less frightened, and even listened to Communists explain that they were on the side of the American people. All American groups worked together now on Red Cross committees, on bond rallies, on blood-bank drives. We were one people united in a common cause.

It is bitter for me to realize that Communist Party leaders looked upon this united front as only a tactic to disrupt this country, and that they were using the good instincts of their own members for their ultimate destruction. Under the deceptive cloak of unity they moved like thieves in the night, stealing materials and secrets. Each Communist Party member was used as a part of the conspiracy, but the majority of them were unaware of it. Only those who knew the pattern knew how each fitted in the picture.

I had stayed close to the Party during the worst days of 1939 to 1941, the days of the Soviet-Nazi pact, primarily because I deeply loved the Teachers Union which I represented. My love for it was no abstract emotion. I felt affection for all its members, the strong and the weak, the arrogant and the humble. I identified myself with them. The kind of sensitivity some people have for their church or their nation I had for the Union. I grew closer to the Party because it was endlessly solicitous of the teachers' problems and gave us favorable publicity and supported our campaigns.

The second reason was because of the Party's campaign

against war. I now know that this anti-war policy was merely a tactic to meet changing conditions. At that time I could not believe that the communist line was a scheme advancing Communists one more step closer to total war for total control of the world. I had slowly come to believe in the infallibility of "scientific socialism" and in the inevitability of the socialist millennium. I was by no means oblivious to many signs of crudeness, corruption, and selfishness within the Party but I thought the movement was a bigger thing.

I, and hundreds like me, believed in Stachel and Foster, Browder and Stalin, and the Politburo, and the great Party of the Soviet Union. We felt they were incorruptible. Blind faith in the Soviet Union, the land of true socialism, was the last spell that was broken for me. This had been a spell woven of words cleverly strung together by Party intellectuals who lied, and it was made plausible by my desire to see man-made perfection in this imperfect world.

During this period Rose Wortis, a woman of the ascetic type, much like Harriet Silverman, self-effacing, devoted, tireless in her work, a willing cog in the machine of professional revolutionaries, was supervising me while I prepared a leaflet for the Women's Trade Union Committee for Peace. I had included a statement against the Nazis, which Rose crossed out as she corrected it, and she said:

"Why do you say that? We do not emphasize that during this period."

I was shocked at this, but, unwilling to believe its implications, I excused it on the ground that she was merely a petty functionary. On a higher level, I was sure, no one would make so gross an error. Later on I had a chance to see the higher level.

I was so completely involved with the Party now that

139

it absorbed all my spare time. Its members were my associates and friends. I had no others.

To this was added one other factor, one not to be minimized: I was rising in importance in this strange world. I had joined as an idealist. Now I was beginning to stay because of the sense of power it gave me, and the chance of participation in significant events.

Like others I had known I was now wearing myself out with devotion and work. I became sharp and critical of those who did not pour themselves as completely into the Party. I still based activity on my own standards of goodness, of honesty, and of loyalty. I failed to understand that the Party in making alliances had nothing whatever to do with these qualities, that it was not out to reform the world, but was bent on making a revolution to control the world. I did not know then that to do so it was ready to use cutthroats, liars, and thieves as well as saints and ascetics. I should have known, however, had I reflected on the implications of Lenin's speech delivered at the Third All-Russian Congress of the Russian Young Communist League on October 2, 1920: "... all our morality is entirely subordinated to the interests of the class struggle of the proletariat."

If, occasionally, I saw things that made me uneasy, I rationalized that the times demanded such actions. Once I was startled from this calm assumption. A group of Party and trade-union leaders met in a private home in Greenwich Village to talk with Earl Browder, then leader of the Communist Party, concerning Vito Marcantonio and his work with the Party, and especially in regard to coming elections. Present were several members of the Politburo and a score of communist union leaders of the A.F. of L. and the CIO.

Marcantonio was in a very special relation to the Communist Party. As a voice in Congress he was indispensable. Because he was a close friend of Mayor LaGuardia he helped give the Party strength. At the same time he provided support for the mayor because he was the latter's personal representative in East Harlem. Through him the mayor retained connections with a section of city politics which no mayor dares overlook. But Marcantonio did not maintain his hold on his congressional district without the Communist Party.

At the meeting we discussed nominations for representative-at-large for New York. Some of us had recommended endorsement of a Republican who had served in the State Senate on the Republican and Labor tickets, a man who had ably represented the East Harlem area. Marcantonio at that time was in alliance with Tammany Hall, and he insisted on the endorsement of a candidate who had a bad voting record and was more often absent from his desk in Congress than present.

In my naïveté I thought that all we had to do was to show the Party leadership his voting record and the Party would support the better-qualified candidate. But the answer to our request was a flat "no" from Browder. We were ordered not to interfere with the decisions of Marcantonio. I sat in utter surprise at this command, for I had believed firmly that Party decisions were arrived at democratically.

Even worse was the next thing to occur. Important trade-union leaders began to complain about what they termed unreasonable demands made on their unions by Marcantonio. When they had finished, Browder told them bluntly that anyone who opposed Marcantonio was expendable. I watched the union leaders listen as the Party leader delivered his edict. They looked like whipped curs. There was a short silence after Browder finished, and I saw these men of importance in their unions begin to explain away their opposition, to laugh nervously about nothing, to accept a decision they had previously sworn they would never accept.

With a sinking heart I accepted it, too, and promptly began to rationalize: it was no doubt all due to some exigency of practical politics about which I knew nothing. The incident, however, left me with a lasting residue of resentment.

In 1942, I myself was thrown into the heart of violent left-wing politics. During the days of the Soviet-Nazi pact the bitterest fight of all was the one between the Social Democrats and the Communists for control of the American Labor Party, which had become the balance of power in New York State.

The Democratic Party could not carry the state without the support of the Labor Party. The Republicans could not carry the state without splitting this new political force. Those trained in the left-wing school of politics were showing an aptitude for practical politics which put the old machine politicians out of the running.

The Social Democrats under the leadership of Alex Rose of the Millinery Union and of David Dubinsky of the Ladies Garment Workers Union had originally collaborated in the building of the American Labor Party. By vying with each other in making alliances with the Democrats and the Republicans for successive elections, each group obtained for its followers certain places on the ballot which would insure election if the joint slate was victorious.

In 1937 and 1939 the combined American Labor Party forces had been successful in getting posts in city and state elections. With the coming of the Soviet-Nazi pact the Social Democrats began a campaign against the Communists both in the unions and in the American Labor Party. Because the Communists had wooed the intellectuals and liberals who were in the Labor Party; because of the Party's alliance with Marcantonio's East Harlem machine (a personal machine); because of Party strength in the new CIO unions, the Party-supported candidates were victorious in several primary fights. Thus they had by 1942 dislodged the Social Democrats from control of the Labor Party in every borough except Brooklyn.

The spring primaries of that year saw a bitter fight between these two factions for the control of Brooklyn. I was established by the Party in headquarters at the Piccadilly Hotel as secretary of a committee, ubiquitously called the Trade Union Committee to Elect Win-the-War candidates. I had the job assigned me of applying the Party whip to various left-wing unions for money, and forces, for the elections.

The committee devoted its energy to two campaigns: to defeat the Dubinsky forces in Brooklyn, and to win the nomination for Marcantonio in all three political parties in his congressional district. He was running in the Republican, Democrat, and Labor party primaries.

The communist wing of the American Labor Party won the primary elections in Brooklyn after a bitter fight which included an appeal to the courts. Marcantonio won the primary in all three parties after the expenditure of incredible sums of money and the utilization of an unbelievable number of union members mobilized by the Party as canvassers in his district.

Every night thousands of men and women combed the East Harlem district house by house. The voters were visited many times. On the first visit they were asked to sign pledges to vote for Marcantonio on a specific party ticket. Next they were reminded by a caller of the date of the primary. And on the day itself they were visited every hour until they went to the polls. Squads of automobiles waited to take them. Teachers acted as baby sitters. People who would have scorned working for a Republican or Democratic leader, willingly and without recompense, did the most menial tasks because the Party had told them that this was the way to defeat the "fascists."

Call it mass hypnosis if you like, but the important thing is to recognize this appeal to the good in human beings and to realize how it can be used.

Hundreds of members of the Teachers Union were assigned to Puerto Rican and Negro districts where they helped people take literacy tests. They manned the polls. They spoke on street corners during the campaign and listened in ecstasy to Marcantonio, who ended all his speeches with "Long live a free Puerto Rico," a rallying cry which had absolutely nothing to do with the primary elections.

By the end of the primary campaign I was exhausted. Yet I went back to the Teachers Union office and worked during the hot summer days to help the skeleton force working there. I think we were the only teacher organization which made a practice of keeping some activity going all summer. We gave social affairs for out-of-town teachers at Columbia and New York University. We serviced the summer schoolteachers and substitutes and we prepared for the coming school term.

In that year the American Labor Party decided to support the Democratic candidate, Jerry Finkelstein, against Frederic Coudert for the State Senate. The Teachers Union responded to the appeal for help. The senatorial district was a peculiar one, consisting of three assembly districts, the famous Greenwich Village Tenth, the silk-stocking Fifteenth, and the Puerto Rican East Harlem Seventeenth.

144

Extremes of wealth and poverty were encompassed in these districts, from fabulous Park Avenue homes to rat- and vermin-infested tenements. The Communist Party released all teacher comrades from other assignments to let them work on this campaign.

I was moved into a suite of offices at the Murray Hill Hotel on Park Avenue and we established a front committee there made up of outstanding citizens. "The Allied Voters Against Coudert" was officially under the chairmanship of a fine and intelligent woman, Mrs. Arthur Garfield Hayes. It included people such as Louis Bromfield, Samuel Barlow, and scores of other respectable people.

One of the attorneys for Amtorg, the Soviet business organization, contributed money and also information helpful to the campaign against Coudert. There was hardly any Democratic organization in the silk-stocking district, and the one in the Village was reputedly tied so closely with the Republicans that we established our own. This left the Democratic organization in East Harlem, which was increasingly under Marcantonio's control, as the key to the election. The contest would be won or lost in that district.

I soon realized that Marcantonio, who had won the primary in all three parties, was not fighting too hard to carry the district for the American Labor Party against Coudert. He did not care which party won; he was the candidate in all three. Besides, Mayor LaGuardia was pledged to do all he could for Senator Coudert and Marcantonio was responsive to the mayor's requests. But Marcantonio promised help, and we made some money available for the leaders of his machine.

My worst fears were confirmed when I listened to the election returns and knew we had lost. I did not mind the loss of the silk-stocking district. But to lose Marcantonio's

145

district was a blow to my faith in individual people in this strange left-wing world.

That night Harry, one of Marc's old captains, drove me home. I was depressed, not only because of the loss of the election, but because of the lesson I had learned. We stopped at the Village Vanguard and there met Tom O'Connor, labor editor of *P.M.*, a good friend of mine, and one of the human people in the Party. He looked at me, but I said nothing. He knew what had happened.

When the Vanguard closed, Tom and I walked downtown to City Hall through the empty streets. We talked of the "movement" and of the strange dead ends it often led to. We talked of the opportunists who cluttered the road to that Mecca of perfection on which we still fixed our eyes.

We walked across Brooklyn Bridge just as dawn was breaking. Tom put me in a taxi. When I reached home, I went to bed and slept twice around the clock.

CHAPTER ELEVEN

The war years made everything seem unreal, even the Party. There was, however, no lack of activity and sometimes the Party had an important part in it.

The leaders of our Teachers Union were unhappy because they were without labor affiliations, therefore I negotiated for affiliation with another communist-led union, the State County and Municipal Workers. We had been Local 5 of the A.F. of L.; now we became Local 555 of the CIO.

The Union set up new headquarters at 13 Astor Place in a building once owned by the Alexander Hamilton Institute and later owned by a corporation controlled by one of the wealthiest communist-led unions, Local 65 of the Warehousemen's Union. It had renamed the building Tom Mooney Hall. Local 65 was renting floors to unions and left-wing organizations. The State County and Municipal Workers were on the seventh floor. The Teachers

Union took over the fifth floor. It gave us plenty of space for professional and social activities.

The Union had assumed the obligation of helping the teachers and professors displaced by the Rapp-Coudert Committee, which was proving difficult to do. Finally, after brooding over this problem, we decided to establish a liberal school for adults, thus making employment and spreading education at the same time.

The School for Democracy was established with Dr. Howard Selsam, formerly of the Philosophy Department of Brooklyn College, as director, and with David Goldway, formerly of Townsend Harris High School and also formerly state director of education for the Communist Party in New York, as secretary. It was to be housed also at 13 Astor Place and to use certain facilities jointly with the Teachers Union. I worked hard to get it organized.

The school was a success. Almost immediately our science teachers received well-paying jobs in experimental laboratories. But the Party observed our venture into education and made ready to bend it to its purposes.

Attached to the Party for some time had been a school called the Workers School, located at Party headquarters. This school was conducted by the Party for members and sympathizers. Its curriculum consisted largely of courses in Marxism-Leninism, courses in trade-union history, and courses in popularizing the current line of the Party. The school was frankly one for communist indoctrination and no compromise was made with bourgeois educational concepts. The school had a foreign atmosphere about it. It was run by old-time Communists, half-affectionately and half-contemptuously referred to as the "Nineteen Fivers."

Earl Browder and the national leadership were busy striving to give the Communist Party the appearance of a native American party to prepare it for its new role in the

148

war and in the postwar period when it was expected to play an even greater role. He was enthusiastic about the School for Democracy.

Often I had the feeling he was impatient with the overwhelming foreignness of the Party. Perhaps his days as child and young man in Kansas had had something to do with it. His slogan, "Communism Is Twentieth Century Americanism," had irked both the foreign-minded Communists and the native Americans who had felt it was an attempt to sell a bogus article. But with the war Browder could work with impunity to convert the Party into an acceptable American social and political organization.

In line with this it was decided to take over the School for Democracy with its core of professors, graduates of the most distinguished bourgeois colleges, and to join it to the hard core of communist teachers from the Workers School. Alexander Trachtenberg was put in charge of a committee to merge the Workers School and the School for Democracy. An astute Communist, a charter member of the Party and before that a revolutionary socialist, Trachtenberg was and is now one of the financial big wheels of the movement. He was also chief of the firm of International Publishers, which had a monopoly on the publication of communist books and pamphlets and on the distribution of Soviet books and pamphlets. This is a highly profitable undertaking.

He bought a beautiful building on the corner of Sixteenth Street and Sixth Avenue, a stone's throw from St. Francis Xavier School, to house the new Marxist School. Plans were already on foot for a string of Marxist Adult Education schools which would have a patriotic look. The patriots of the American Revolution and of the Civil War were to be given a new sort of honor — a Marxist status. The new school in New York was named the Jefferson

School of Social Research. In Chicago the school was named the Abraham Lincoln School, in Boston the John Adams School, and in New Rochelle, the Thomas Paine School. These schools were to play a part in the "third revolution" that was to destroy the nation.

Trachtenberg once said to me that when communism came to America it would come under the label of "progressive democracy." "It will come," he added, "in labels acceptable to the American people."

The initial funds for the setting up of the Marxist schools were, ironically enough, contributed by wealthy business people who were personally invited to attend dinners at the homes of other men of wealth. They came to hear Earl Browder analyze current events and predict the future with emphasis on the role the Party would play.

There is no doubt that Earl Browder, as chief of the Communist Party, was close to the seats of world power in those days, and that he knew better than most Americans what was going on, except insofar as events were warped and refracted by his Marxist ideology. The men who paid their hundred-dollar admissions and contributed thus to the school funds became part of the group which Earl Browder was to call the "progressive businessmen," meaning those who were willing to go along on an international program of communism. The lure was attractive: expanded profits from trade with the Soviets. The price to be paid was unimportant to these well-fed, well-heeled men, who felt the world was their oyster. The price was respectability for communism at home and leadership of the Soviets abroad.

I had no part in the group which planned this new Marxist educational empire, though I had been the moving spirit in establishing the School for Democracy. The trustees of the Jefferson School were not educators; they

150

were key communist figures in the growing hierarchy of a native American leadership for the Communist Party. There were among them people with unbelievable backgrounds, some of them Moscow-trained, but they all had a surface of respectability, even though sometimes a blurred surface.

As I look back I see that I never ceased keeping for myself a small area of freedom into which my mind could escape. Some phases of my life I was perfectly willing to have controlled and even enslaved. I was conditioned to accept the view that the capitalist system was inefficient, greedy, immoral, and decadent. My schools and my reading and the depression had put me in agreement with President Roosevelt in wanting to drive the money-changers from the Temple. I was also willing to follow the Party in its program of practical politics, for here, too, the attack was upon the grossness and stupidity of those in government who sat in the seats of power with no plan for the future. Willingly, too, I helped the Party gain in power in the field of American education through my work with the Teachers Union. I was always ready to help in the struggle for admission to the academic world of the intellectuals among our immigrant population who felt they faced discrimination.

But I was wary of the Party's inner educational apparatus. I was not drawn to the dogmatic pedants of the Party's schools. No doubt, subconsciously, I realized that all this was not education but propaganda, and at heart I was really still a student and a teacher. I wanted to read Marx and Engels and Lenin, but not under the tutelage of those drab, self-effacing figures who peopled the Party's educational quarters.

The Party leaders made frequent attempts to get me to attend state and national training schools. I was ap-

151

proached repeatedly about the possibility of going to school in Moscow, but I always pleaded that the immediate emergencies of my work in the Union made it impossible for me to give time to such a duty. "Perhaps someday," I told them.

I had seen teachers, sailors, furriers, subway conductors, housewives, some with third-grade education and some with college degrees, lumped together as students in these state and national training schools and I had seen them come out with the same stamp of dedicated uniformity. It was a leveling process that still gave them an odd sense of superiority, as if they were now priests of a new cult.

With the development of the new Marxist schools I tended to withdraw further from this phase of the work. I taught one class at the Jefferson School, but I found no joy in it. When I was offered the directorship of the California Labor School I refused it without hesitation. I had the vague fear that if I allowed myself to be drawn into this type of indoctrination the last small refuge where my mind found freedom would be gone.

The war years had produced interesting phenomena in communist-led left-wing circles, not the least of which was public renunciation of the class struggle. The Party announced that whole sections of the capitalist class had joined the "democratic front," the so-called "Roosevelt camp of progress."

The *Daily Worker* never wearied of enumerating those who were clasping hands in a common purpose, Communists, trade unions, sections of the Democratic Party, and progressive capitalists. These made a coalition, the Party stated, that would win the war and later the peace.

The Communist Party now assumed the responsibility for establishing a rigid discipline over the working class. No employer was more effective or more relentless in

152

checking strikes among the workers, or in minimizing complaints of workers against inequities of wages and working conditions. Some employers were delighted with this assistance. It is startling to note that, while wages rose a little during those years, they did not compare with the rise in profits and in monopoly control of basic necessities.

In other circumstances, Communists would have blasted the fact that war production was chiefly in the hands of ten large corporations and that 80 per cent of the war production was in the hands of a hundred firms. Now the Communists carefully muted such information. Instead, they played on the workers' feelings of patriotism.

It was sad to observe that in the interest of its objectives the Party even barred the protests of the Negro workers who felt that, now that they were needed in the war factories, they might win some rights. The Communists opposed the Negro demands violently. In fact, a campaign of vilification was begun. It was charged that the leaders of this Negro movement were Japanese agents.

The Party did all it could to induce women to go into industry. Its fashion designers created special styles for them and its song writers wrote special songs to spur them. Use of womanpower in the war industries was, of course, inevitable, but it also fitted into the communist long-range program. War-period conditions, they planned, were to become a permanent part of the future educational program. The bourgeois family as a social unit was to be made obsolete.

After the Teheran conference, the Party program for shelving strikes was projected into a permanent no-strike policy. Each time American political leaders emerged from an international conference, Crimea, Teheran, and Yalta, the Communist Party announced again its dedica-

153

tion to the win-the-war plan. Its leaders were driving for a strong war and peace unity between the United States and the Soviet Union. Everywhere the Party leadership was being placed in positions of importance so that they might direct the home-front segments of the coalition. Communist leadership was being consulted and utilized by those in power in government.

The drive for the second front brought Earl Browder into national prominence, and we realized that he was being consulted by such national leaders as Sumner Welles. Government officials were utilizing Communists to pull together divergent groups.

When the Russian War Relief was begun, a glittering array of names of outstanding citizens adorned its elegant stationery. Sumptuous affairs launched Russian relief in America. These were attended by people prominent in society and government.

The Communist Party made the most of this. Now there emerged the Russian Institute with its imposing headquarters on Park Avenue. This was a sophisticated propaganda agency; it brought American educators, public officials, artists, young people of families of wealth into this left-wing world. Famous names, Vanderbilt, Lamont, Whitney, Morgan, mingled with those of communist leaders. The Russian Institute was so respectable that it was allowed to give in-service courses to New York City schoolteachers for credit.

In Albany and in Washington a new crop of young, native American Communists swarmed into the legislative halls as legislative representatives and public-relation and research aides to legislators. With inside information on what was happening, they were able to guide legislators in the direction of Soviet-American unity. They helped to produce dozens of important public figures at Madison

Square Garden rallies, organized under various labels but filled by the rank and file of devoted Party members. It was a glittering society that was emerging, made up of Russian diplomats and Russian business agents, of Americans in evening clothes, and artistic Bohemians in careless dungarees, all of them cheering the repeated avowals of friendship with the Soviet Motherland.

When in 1943 Stalin announced the dissolution of the Communist International, a great impetus was given to the drive to build the Communist Party into a native American party. This dissolution was a tactic meant to lessen fear in those Americans who did not believe that Soviet-American unity could be achieved without danger to American sovereignty.

When I arrived in Albany for the legislative session of 1943 I was besieged with questions. Everywhere I explained the new policy of peace, the new era that was coming to the world because of this communist policy of amity. When some days later I spoke at a budget hearing to a packed hall, ostensibly for my Union, I was in reality putting across the Party's unity line in terms of the taxation problem. I received congratulations from Republicans, Democrats, and representatives of the taxpayers' organization.

Afterward Gil Green, New York State chairman of the Communist Party, and Si Gerson, its legislative representative, congratulated me on my speech. Then Gil said decidedly: "The time has come, Bella, when you ought to come forward openly as a leader of the Party." Si Gerson, he added, was going into the Army soon and there would be need of a new legislative representative of the Party. "And we want you."

We had supper in the grill at the De Witt Clinton Hotel and there we were joined by CIO men, by local labor lawyers, and a representative of the Farmers Union. My favorite waiter, a Party member, took our order. I was only half-listening to the talk of the people milling around our table, for Gil Green had startled me by his abrupt suggestion, which I knew was almost a command. I liked Gil. He wore shabby, worn suits and he reminded me of Harriet Silverman and Rose Wortis and the other self-sacrificing, dedicated people.

In the Party I was beginning to see many people of a different stripe. During the war period I saw how opportunism and selfishness engulfed many comrades. They wore expensive clothes, lived in fine apartments, took long vacations at places provided by men of wealth. There was, for one, William Wiener, former treasurer of the Party, manipulator for a score of business enterprises, who wore Brooks Brothers suits, smoked expensive cigars, and lunched only at the best places. There were the trade-union Communists who rubbed elbows with underworld characters at communist-financed night clubs, and labor lawyers who were given patronage by the Party by assignment to communist-led trade unions and now were well established and comfortable.

But it was shabby, serious-faced Gil Green who was for me a visible reassurance that the Communist Party was still what I had originally thought it. His proposal had come to me at a time when I was tired of the varying grades of protection which the Party gave to its members, and tired of seeing the comfortable way of life of some who were in powerful places, where they had the support of the Party but faced none of the disadvantages of belonging to it.

Before I left him I promised Gil that I would think seriously about his proposal. I had personal problems to consider if I took it, for it was in a way an irrevocable step.

For one thing, I would be giving up a certain area of freedom, since I would be giving up fields of work not open to an avowed Communist.

In everything except name I was a Communist. I accepted discipline and attended meetings. I gave a full measure of devotion to Party works, and I felt a deep attachment and loyalty to the people in its ranks. I considered myself as part of a group looking and driving toward the day when socialism would triumph.

Even more significant was the fact that I had made their hates my hates. This was what established me as a full-fledged Communist. In the long ago I had been unable to hate anyone; I suffered desperately when someone was mistreated; I was regarded as a peacemaker. Now, little by little, I had acquired a whole mass of people to hate: the groups and individuals who fought the Party. How it came about I cannot tell. All I know as I look back to that time is that my mind had responded to Marxist conditioning. For it is a fact, true and terrible, that the Party establishes such authority over its members that it can swing their emotions now for and now against the same person or issue. It claims such sovereignty even over conscience as to dictate when it shall hate.

Before 1935, for instance, the Party had preached hatred of John L. Lewis as a labor dictator. No stories about him were too vile. He was accused of murder and pillage in his march to power in the Miners Union. Suddenly, in 1936, Lewis became the hero of the Communist Party. Again in 1940, when the Party decided to support Roosevelt against Willkie, and John L. Lewis risked his leadership in the CIO by calling on the unions to vote for Willkie, the Communists screamed invective, and in private meetings Roy Hudson and William Z. Foster, in charge of labor for the Politburo, vilified Lewis. When the Communists

157

shifted their support, Lewis was dropped as president of the CIO and Philip Murray was elected in his place.

During my years in the Teachers Union I gradually got used to these bitter expressions of hate. And since hate begets hate, often those under attack also responded with hate. Hearing them, I began to take sides and in the end accepted the Party's hates as my own.

Once at the national convention of the American Federation of Teachers in 1938 I was assigned to attack a resolution introduced by the socialists in support of a Fred Beals, once a Communist, and indicted for murder in the Gastonia textile strike. He had jumped bail and escaped to Russia but he did not like life in the Soviet Union and insisted on returning to the United States even though it meant standing trial. The socialists were defending him and asking trades-union support for him because the indictment had grown out of a labor dispute.

I did not know Fred Beals, and from a purely labor point of view I should have been sympathetic. Instead, I accepted the assignment to speak against the resolution to help him. I had begun to adopt the hates of a group.

This is the peculiar paradox of modern totalitarianism. This is the key to the mental enslavement of mankind: that the individual is made into nothing, that he operates as the physical part of what is considered a higher group intelligence and acts at the will of that higher intelligence, that he has no awareness of the plans the higher intelligence has for utilizing him. When a person conditioned by a totalitarian group talks about the right not to incriminate himself, he really means the right not to incriminate the communist group of which he is only a nerve end. When he talks of freedom of speech, he means freedom for the communist group to speak as a group through the mouth of the individual who has been selected by the higher intelligence.

158

The Bill of Rights of the American Constitution was written to protect individuals against centralized power. The Communists pervert this safeguard by first enslaving the individual so that he becomes the marionette of the centralized power.

This kind of conditioning had something to do with my decision to become a card-carrying Communist. In March, 1943, I gave my consent to Gil Green's proposal to become an open Party leader. I took over Si Gerson's position as legislative representative for the New York district. Gil was pleased and insisted that I begin the transition immediately, so I spent some time in Party headquarters and attended all meetings.

Now I found myself faced with two tasks: to prepare myself for my new life, and to effect an orderly withdrawal from the Teachers Union.

For several years I had purposely helped to bring forward new Party members for posts of responsibility in the Teachers Union leadership. One of these was Rose Russell, who had taught French in Thomas Jefferson High School. Rose had a fine mind and had had some training in newspaper work. She had a human approach to people and problems. She was not as yet stamped into the obvious Communist Party mold. She was personable and well-liked, and the old guard in the Party fraction in the Union would not, I knew, dare oppose her openly. She was my choice as successor to the post I had loved, and with the approval of Gil and Rose Wortis we got the necessary approval by the communist leadership of the teachers. It was then an easy matter to bring her forth as a candidate for the Union elections of 1944.

Technically I was to remain as the legislative representative of the Teachers Union until the elections were held and until Rose Russell was installed publicly. The Union gave a farewell affair in my honor in June 1944. It was a fine illustration of the kind of unity which this Union, now a sturdy arm of the Communist Party, was able to establish.

The farewell party was called "A Tribute to Dear Bella." As I read today the blurbs on the program I can but shake my head sadly. I read there of the "inspiring and untiring leadership in behalf of all the children — all the teachers — the improvement in public education — the fight against racial intolerance." The chairman was my old friend, Professor Margaret Schlauch of New York University.

Telegrams were read from scores of assemblymen and state senators, from trade-union leaders, both communist and noncommunist, congressmen, and judges. On the platform were outstanding leaders come to honor me, for I had won many of these people to a tolerance for the Union by a sincere espousal of the needs of the schools. Among the people who greeted me were Charles Hendley, Honorable Hulan Jack, then in the Assembly, and Judge Anna Kross, whom I had grown to respect and love.

Rose Russell presented me with a gift from the Union, a modernistic water color which still hangs on my law-office wall. It is a good reminder, in its complete confusion of subject matter, of the distortion of the actual, the confusion and meaninglessness of this part of my life.

CHAPTER TWELVE

I HAD NOW BECOME an elder statesman of the Teachers Union. I retained my membership as an honorary member and at the direction of the Party I remained on the top communist committee. I helped Rose Russell establish her leadership and I tried to pass on to her what I had learned over the years. I introduced her to the public officials with whom I had worked. She did not have to face the hostility I met when first I went to Albany, for the Party had grown in power, and the organization it controlled was sending many representatives to Albany. The Party now had allies among the lobbyists, the legislators, and the press correspondents. I was in Albany frequently as the representative of the Communist Party and was able to spend much time with Rose.

The previous year my husband obtained a divorce down South. Shortly thereafter I heard he had remarried. These events and the death of my mother led me to immerse myself more completely than ever in my work for the

Union and the Party. However, I missed a personal family life and I often talked of adopting children. But the comrades dissuaded me. They reminded me I could not overcome the legal handicaps of adoption for a woman living alone, and I knew, too, that irregular hours and my limited income would make it difficult. Instead, I continued to move in a world of men who were determined to create new types of human beings who would conform to the blueprint of the world they confidently expected to control. I lived only as part of an ideological group. I was accepted by them and I dealt with them in the direct but impersonal manner I had long cultivated.

In March 1943 I began to spend part of each day at Party headquarters at 35 East Twelfth Street. This building, which ran from Twelfth Street to Thirteenth Street, was owned by the Party. On the first floor was the Workers' Bookshop and entrance to the freight and passenger elevators that served the whole building. The third floor housed the New York County apparatus. The fourth was used to store the books of the International Publishing Company. The fifth held the New York State leadership. The sixth had the publication offices of the Yiddish paper, the *Freiheit*, and the Jewish Commission. The seventh and eighth floors were used by the *Daily Worker*. On the ninth floor was the headquarters of the national leadership of the Party.

Despite a campaign to clean up the building, it remained unbelievably drab. For a long time the Communists had resisted any attempt to beautify the place because that was regarded as bourgeois pretentiousness. The only pictures on the walls were those of Lenin, Marx, and Stalin. The only decorations were Red flags.

Under the impetus of Browder's attempt to make the Communist Party American, a cleanup job was begun.

The walls got new paint. New photographs of the American leadership appeared. I came on the scene just after the painting was completed — a ghastly cream with brown trim. Lenin and Stalin got equal space on the walls and the photographs of the members of the Politburo, each exactly identical in size and type of frames, were placed in identical positions, none lower, none higher than the other. They ranged high along the walls of the ninth floor. Looking at them, I had the feeling I was entering the abode of some strange secret cult, and I was both attracted and repelled.

Daily as I entered my office on the fifth floor gates and doors were opened and then locked by strange, silent men and women. At first the excessive precaution surprised me, but I was to learn that many of the people who entered that center of intrigue needed protection.

I went to several meetings of the Politburo with Gil Green. There I found Earl Browder, William Z. Foster, Bob Minor, Jim Ford, Jack Stachel, John Williamson, and Elizabeth Gurly Flynn in attendance. Browder seemed the undisputed leader, but the others did not seem coerced or intimidated, as later they testified they had been. The meetings were like meetings of a board of directors, one in which all conformed willingly.

As I began to prepare for the work I was assigned to do I was amazed at the lack of files of material on social questions such as housing and welfare. When I complained about this, Gil said: "Bella, we are a revolutionary party, not a reform group. We aren't trying to patch up this bourgeois structure."

I began to realize why the Party had no long-range program for welfare, hospitals, schools, or child care. They plagiarized programs from the various civil-service unions. Such reforms, if they fitted in, could be adapted to the taste of the moment. But reforms were anathema to communist long-range strategy, which stood instead for revolution and dictatorship of the proletariat.

The Party wanted me to retain my contacts with the non-communist world, which had been so easy while I represented the Teachers Union, but which I knew would be difficult as an avowed Communist. Gil was delighted when I discussed the possibility of establishing a law office midtown which I could use to meet non-Party friends of the Party who would not go to the Party headquarters for fear of police surveillance. I set up business with two young lawyers who wanted to practice in the labor field. They thought that my growing power in left-wing politics would aid them.

So Philip Jones, Allen Goodwin, and I found suitable offices at 25 West Forty-third Street. We established the firm and got off to a good start. But I found little time for the practice of law. My office became a place where I met Party and non-Party persons engaged in common enterprises.

Earl Browder was then preparing for the Party convention of 1944. At this convention I was to make the public announcement of my Party affiliation. Gil told me that they were preparing a list of close to a hundred trade unionists who would also join the Party openly at the same time.

Like many of the liaison agents of the Party, I now began spending hours in restaurants and cafeterias, meeting with Party people from all walks of life, explaining, urging, cajoling, telling them what to do and what was expected of them.

That spring of 1943 was memorable for the new friends I met. I had moved to an apartment on Seventh Avenue near Fourteenth Street. The rent was small for it was over a restaurant. Nevertheless it was a pleasant flat which could easily be shared for it had two rooms in front and two in back and a kitchen and bath in between.

Before long I had a roommate. Through Blackie Myers, vice-president of the National Maritime Union and his wife Beth McHenry, a writer for the *Daily Worker,* I met Nancy Reed, who had recently been fired, with much publicity, from a New York State Labor Department job because of exposure of her communist activity, by Godfrey P. Schmidt, then Deputy Industrial Commissioner. The press carried, as a result of the investigations of Stephen Birmingham, lurid stories of how she had buried Communist Party records in the sand at her mother's summer home on Cape Cod. She was out of a job. I offered to share my apartment, and then persuaded the Teachers Union to set up an employment bureau and to make her its director.

Nancy came from a good Boston family. I knew her mother, Ferdinanda Reed, who was one of the three old ladies who technically owned the *Daily Worker,* the other two being Anita Whitney and my former tenant in the Village, Susan Woodruff. Ferdinanda had come to communism intellectually and remained because, like Susan, she never saw its ruthless side. Her two daughters had followed her into the Party and Nancy's sister Mary, a writer of some note, had left her American husband and taken their infant son and gone to Russia to live. Nancy had visited her there.

Nancy had many friends among the working people for whom she had helped find jobs when she worked for the State Employment Bureau. Also she had great vitality and a love for social life. When I came home at night I found our apartment swarming with people. Some were from the civil-service unions. Many of them were men from the ships, for among her closest friends were Ted Lewis,

165

vice-president of the National Maritime Union, Joseph Curran, Ferdinand Smith, and others of the union leadership. The seamen during those war days were earning good wages, for there were overtime bonuses and special allotments for war risk.

Before I knew it my home became a center for National Maritime Union leaders and seamen of every rank. Among them came Captain Mulzac, the first Negro to become a captain, and scores of engineers, chief stewards, pumpmen, boatswains, and ordinary seamen. Some came only for a single party, but others were regular visitors.

One evening John Rogan of the National Maritime Union brought a tall, slender, red-haired seaman in khaki shirt and trousers who had been a friend of Paddy Whalen. "Red," as his friends called him, proved a fine addition to the party for he talked well and had many stories to tell. He came from Minnesota. He said his grandmother was the first white woman in that state. As he talked of his people you knew he was proud of his heritage. His mother was a French Canadian, a convent-bred girl, and he said he, too, was raised a Catholic. His grandfather from Wisconsin had been killed at the battle of Shiloh and was buried in Springfield, Illinois.

I told him of my former husband's grandfather who fought with the South and lost an arm in that battle. We talked late into the night and I learned that he had left his Church and become an IWW and had worked with the Communist Party at times. I told him proudly of my recent decision to become an open worker in the Party. Dubiously, he asked, "Are you sure that is what you want?" and as I looked surprised, he continued:

"You see, I don't think they have the answer. I simply can't make myself believe that we are only clods of earth and that when we die, we die and that's all. I've seen bad

166

conditions in lots of places, on ships, in jails, and in foreign ports in China and India and Africa and South America. I've fought against these conditions. There's no doubt that out of it all revolution may come — the way the Communists want it to — but what will come after that? What will this crowd do when they've got their revolution? I hate to think about it. But I'm pretty sure they haven't got the answer."

I was startled to hear this sort of talk from a man who had stubbornly worked and fought for labor, often with a reckless disregard for the safety of his life. He was not a "class enemy." As he talked, I sensed the uneasy feeling that sometimes came over me, even though I tried to ignore it. It was as if this man's words were the echo of my own unformulated fears.

But they did not alter my decision to be formally inducted into the Party leadership. For years I had functioned with the Party without a Party card or other formal indication of allegiance. Now Gil Green gave me my first Party card, and when he asked to which branch I wanted to be assigned I named the section in East Harlem. To become effective in that area I now moved to a house on upper Lexington Avenue, a neighborhood that had once been Irish and where there still remained a scattering of Irish and Italian families, but where there were an increasing number of Puerto Rican, West Indian, and Negro families. I called our block the street of all nations.

On the corner of 102d Street was a Negro Episcopal church and I became a good friend of the minister and his family. Next to it was a Puerto Rican boardinghouse run by an Italian spinster. Nearby was a grocery store owned by an Irishman from the old country, who spoke with a brogue. We all lived together in peace as good neighbors.

I gave one floor in my house to Clotilda McClure and her

husband Jim. Mrs. McClure had worked for me in the early days of my marriage when we lived at the house on Eleventh Street. I was happy to have them in the house because we were good friends and also because Clotilda helped me with the care of the house.

I had moved into this particular neighborhood because, as a Party functionary, I wanted to work in this community and I wished to study its special problems. I was assigned to the Garibaldi Branch of the Party located on 116th Street, a Party club which concentrated on recruiting Italians. The club was ineffective and drab, due in part to the fact that Italians in America were loath to join the Communist Party and in part also to Vito Marcantonio, who represented the American Labor Party and actively worked for the Communist Party. But he did not relish a strong local Communist Party in his district, perhaps because he thought it might get in his way when he made fast deals with the diverse forces.

His own center of political activity was a brownstone clubhouse on 116th Street near Second Avenue. There congregated a strange assortment of smooth, sophisticated communist boys and girls, going and coming in the game of political intrigue, members of local gangs, known racketeers, ambitious lawyers, and political opportunists looking for the crumbs of his political favor.

There were also people of the neighborhood who needed a friend. Marc listened to their stories, assigned lieutenants to their cases, or called on communist-led unions for help. He wrote his people many letters from Washington on his letterhead as Representative. Nothing made these simple people so happy as to receive one of his letters from the capital, and they carried them in their pockets and displayed them proudly. It did not matter even if the letter said nothing; the fact that they knew a congressman who wrote them a letter was enough. He could have been elected on a Wooden Indian ticket by these people for they belonged to no party. They followed Marc as a personality.

The Garibaldi branch of the Communist Party was a block from his club. This branch of fifty or sixty members consisted chiefly of Italians, Jews, Negroes, and Finns. Some of the Italians were old-time anarchists. Yet they felt at home with the Communists if only because of their atheism and belief in violence. I found plenty of work to do in East Harlem, but I soon learned that the Labor Party and its activees, the Communists, were concerned mainly about getting out the vote. Certainly they were not concerned about the welfare of the people. This was a new type of political machine, attracting not only the voters but the actual precinct workers by vague promises of future social betterment.

By January 1944 I was firmly established at Party headquarters on Twelfth Street. There I organized the legislative program of the Party; but, more important still, I supervised the legislative work of the unions, chiefly the unions of government workers on a state, local, and national level, of the mass organizations of women, and of the youth organizations.

All over the building there was a noticeable feeling of excitement and optimism. Browder's book, *Victory and After*, placed communist participation in the mainstream of American life, and there was among us less and less left-wing talk and activity. At a state board meeting Gil gave a talk on the new era at hand, and startled us with perspectives new to those who had been brought up on Lenin's thesis that imperialism is the last stage of capitalism. Gil now said that the age of imperialism had come to an end, that Teheran had canceled out Munich, and that

169

Soviet-American unity would continue indefinitely after the war. Together, he added, the United States and the Soviet would solve the world's colonial problems and indeed all other world problems.

Through December, 1943, we at headquarters had heard nothing but Teheran. What had happened at that conference was by no means clear to us. We did know that Browder was writing another book dealing with it. We also knew that Teheran was now the password, that it meant maximum co-operation of Communists with all groups and all classes. The political line which for two years had been called the "Democratic Front" now became the "National Front." That Christmas Teheran did cancel out Bethlehem for us.

The artists and writers who followed the Communists began to interpret Teheran in their work. For every activity Teheran was the key. Huge murals commemorated it as well as café society songs and political skits. For some time this line brought a pleasant sense of security, but by January we heard rumblings of trouble from the ninth floor as they prepared for the coming Party convention.

Dissension had arisen among the leaders. Sam Darcy, the Party organizer from California, disagreed with the proposed change of the Party line and Gil announced at a New York State Board meeting the Politburo decision to expel Darcy, a decision with which he obviously agreed. Strong support of Browder by Gil was no surprise, for we all looked on Gil as Browder's henchman and his choice to succeed him.

A vote was taken supporting the action of the national Politburo to expel Darcy. Like all votes in the Communist Party, it was unanimous. I was startled by the anger displayed against this man who, Gil said, refused to throw aside "revolutionary dogma" to meet a new situation.

170

Only a few days before they had all called him "comrade."

With the expulsion of the dissident Darcy, peace reigned again. We heard that William Z. Foster had also been critical of the proposed change. Nevertheless he had bowed to the majority. And we came together at the convention of 1944 with a rising Party membership and growing prestige for Browder in national politics. We were confident of the Party's importance in the current American scene. We knew Browder was on the inside track on news of the war from overseas and from Washington.

The convention that year was held at Riverside Plaza, a hotel on West Seventy-second Street. It was well attended. Besides the delegates, many trade-union leaders and men of national reputation were there. The Communist International had been, at Roosevelt's insistence, technically dissolved the previous year, but several of its members were in New York and came to our convention. From France, Lucien Midol brought a letter from the Central Committee of the French Communist Party, approving the new American line. There were a few grumbling old-time trade unionists who did not like the new trend and one said sarcastically, "This is the convention in which the workers and the bosses become bedfellows."

My own role, as I have said earlier, was to announce publicly my adherence to the Party. In this I was to be joined by about a hundred trade unionists. When the time came, almost all candidates chosen had found urgent reasons for not making a public declaration. In the end only two, and these from insignificant unions, joined me in becoming open Party members.

The first evening of the convention brought tragic news: Anna Damon had jumped to her death from the window of a nearby hotel. An important auxiliary member of the Politburo, Anna was the daughter of a wealthy Chicago family. She was assigned to work with Charles Ruthenberg, the first secretary of the American Communist Party, and had come East after his death when the Party shifted its headquarters to New York. Here she exercised a powerful influence over the rising Party leadership. She was reputed to have developed for the Party such figures as Earl Browder, Roy Hudson, Charles Krumbein, and others of the Politburo.

I had first met her in the thirties when she was executive secretary of the powerful International Labor Defense, a mass organization with great financial resources and wide contacts with the legal profession. This was the committee which organized communist participation in the Scottsboro and Herndon cases, and in the Gastonia and other labor strikes.

A friend took me one evening to her home on East Sixteenth Street and I remember my amazement that a Communist Party member should be living in such a lavish apartment, with fine paintings and a terrace that looked out over the city and the East River. Marcantonio, over whom she also had great influence and whom she had trained in left-wing politics, was there that evening, and so were Robert Minor and his wife. Everyone except Marc wore evening clothes. When we left, I said a little thoughtfully to the friend who had brought me, "This could be the new aristocracy of our country."

Why Anna Damon killed herself I never learned. The rumors were that she had broken with Browder on the new policy. The Party carefully spread the impression that she had cancer and had taken this way out of pain. But the beginning of a convention of a Party in which she had great power was a strange time to choose for her exit from life — if indeed she did take her own life.

At this convention Earl Browder's speech calling for the dissolution of the Communist Party was, next to Anna's suicide, the most surprising event. Some old-time functionaries could not understand it. Some pretended to see in it an attempt to cancel out the teachings of Lenin.

But the Party machine worked with planned precision. The American Communist Party dissolved itself and then by another resolution the delegates re-established it under the name of the Communist Political Association, with the same leaders, same organization, same friends.

I was elected as a member of the National Committee of this Communist Political Association, which brought me into its top leadership. I was now supposedly a part of the inner circle.

The new change of name puzzled many both in and out of the Party. I had listened closely during the convention and it was not at all clear to me. I knew, of course, that one immediate reason was to lay the basis for leadership of the Communists for the re-election of Roosevelt, since Earl Browder was the first to call publicly for his re-election to a fourth term. I also knew that the new name had a less ominous sound to American ears. Even so, it had been a drastic thing to do.

By those who thought they knew the reason it was explained to me thus: the current line in world communism was now based on the Roosevelt pledge to the Soviet Union of mutual co-existence and continued postwar Soviet-American unity. If that pledge were kept and if the march to world communist control could be achieved by a diplomatic unity arising out of official Soviet-American relations, then there would be no need of a militant class-struggle party. In that case the Communist Political Association would become a sort of Fabian Society, doing research and engaging in promoting social, economic, and political ideas to direct America's development into a full-fledged socialist nation.

The convention over, we turned to the most important

173

item on the Party's agenda, the re-election of President Roosevelt for a fourth term. For this end the National Committee met immediately after the convention. Browder proposed that the Party contribute five thousand dollars to help develop the Willkie Memorial, no doubt as a gesture of amity to the Social Democrats who were also intent on this election. But David Dubinsky and others in charge of the project of building Freedom House as a memorial to Wendell Willkie refused the offer publicly. After that the Communist Political Association moved independently in its self-appointed task of promoting a Roosevelt victory.

It was necessary first to bring the various districts and subdivisions of the organization to quick acceptance of the decision of the convention. Each of us on the National Committee attended little secret meetings, spoke to the comrades, explained the new perspectives, made them feel they were right at the heart of the important things that were going on.

We highlighted Browder's astuteness and our confidence in him and told how prominent people outside the Party agreed with us in this. This was true, for his perspicacity had been praised by Walter Lippman and other publicists. He was praised also for the new constitution of the Communist Political Association, written in conformity with American-type organizations, and for the change from foreign communist terminology, such as "Politburo," to American expressions such as "national board."

Some of us knew, however, that though Browder was Americanizing the appearance of the organization he was having difficulties, because of numerous professional revolutionaries who could not change their speech, manner, and way of thinking so swiftly.

My duties were various. I continued to exercise control over the communist teachers. Before I had left the Union

174

I had been able to lay the basis for affiliation of the Teachers Union with the NEA. In June 1944 I was assigned to speak at a meeting of more than five hundred communist teachers and their friends at the Jefferson School on the new communist perspectives as applied to education. I held out the prospect of a new approach to education soon to be disclosed by American leaders who controlled the purse strings of the nation. I urged the communist teachers to exercise their influence for unity on all teachers' and citizens' groups.

I pointed out that the NAM had established a tie with the NEA and had pledged itself to help build education and to support a nationwide school-building program; that this would grow into a program of continued co-operation on all educational subjects. To those who questioned this perspective I said that the progressive businessmen were playing a revolutionary role. I repeated the explanations given by Gil and other leaders of the new National Board.

As an official member of the New York State Board of the Party and on the state committee, I was second to Gil Green in charge of political campaigns. I was assigned two immediate tasks: the defeat of Hamilton Fish in the Twenty-ninth Congressional District and the building of a New York division of the progressive farmers and businessmen for the re-election of Roosevelt.

The story of communist manipulation for the defeat of Hamilton Fish is too long to tell here. In the other task I was to see for the first time how a tiny minority, well organized, with members in both majority parties, and within trade unions, and with control of small labor parties, could serve as a brain to do what larger groups of unco-ordinated citizens could not do. In this election the Communists served as the major co-ordinating factor.

In the little town of Catskill, on a bright June Sunday

of 1944, a handful of chicken farmers from Sullivan, Columbia, and Orange counties met with an organizer of the Farmers Union, Gil, myself, and Charles Coe, a silent chubby man who was associated with a farmers' publication. Together we planned a Progressive Farmers Committee for the re-election of Roosevelt. Some months later, when the campaign was in full swing, few knew from what small beginnings the large-scale work among the farmers had begun.

In New York the CIO Political Action Committee was staffed with many sophisticated Communists with years of experience in the nation's capital. The Independent Committee of Artists, Scientists and Professionals, under the chairmanship of Jo Davidson, the sculptor, was under strong Party direction.

These election committees, made up of Communists and non-Communists, were under communist control. If the chairman of the committee was a non-Communist, its executive secretary was inevitably under communist domination.

New York, because of its large voting power, was the directive center of the campaign. Press releases from New York, enlarged on by the leading New York papers, set the line for hundreds of newspapers and radio stations in the hinterland.

For the success of this election the American Labor Party moved into high gear. The New Liberal Party, organized by Alex Rose and David Dubinsky, along with George Counts and John Childs, also played an important role. This latter group differentiated itself from the Communists and often attacked them. In reply the Communists moved into action. They wanted all the credit for achieving the election victory, so they took time out to attack Dubinsky and the newly formed Liberal Party, even though they were on the same side in the election campaign.

In that campaign the Communists were everywhere. We did not trust the district leaders of the Democratic Party to deliver the votes, so we sent bright young left-wingers into the Democratic clubhouses to jog the old fellows into action, and it was amusing to see them in that rough-and-tumble atmosphere.

To gather in the votes which the Labor Party could not win and which the Democratic organizations might fail to reach, we set up a National Citizens Political Action Committee. This loose organization held local rallies and collected funds. Its executive committee had many glittering names. The real work was done by the same dedicated little people, the ones who were looking for no personal reward save the right of participation in the building of a new world.

It was fascinating to see how easily the Party personnel acclimated itself to its new role of pulling all forces together. They rubbed elbows with district leaders, with underworld characters, and with old-line political bosses whom they really regarded as caretakers of a disintegrating political apparatus.

While I was in active work I was reasonably happy, but when the campaign was over and Roosevelt re-elected, I found myself depressed. One reason was a peculiar struggle for power which I saw emerging. During the election I had seen effective work done by Communists who were concealed members. Disputes began to develop between open communist functionaries and these concealed Communists who were safely ensconced in well-paid jobs in powerful organizations. These disputes were resolved by Browder himself, if necessary, and always in favor of the concealed members. I felt a growing competition between these groups, and I wanted to run away from it.

One day I spoke about it to Elizabeth Gurly Flynn who was with me on both National and State Committees. She said that it was only in New York that the comrades acted like that. She explained it was often due to male chauvinism at headquarters.

"Go and see a little of the rest of the country," she advised me. "That will make you feel better."

So in 1945 I substituted for her at communist gatherings in the Middle West. From my first talk I realized there was resistance among workers to the new line on co-operation and unity. Many did not like a postwar "no strike pledge," or adoption of a labor-management charter proposed by the Chamber of Commerce and supported by the Communists. The new line was unacceptable to skeptical workers who had been schooled in the class-struggle philosophy and who were at that time feeling the effects of the greed of the powerful monopolies. These were reducing wages, and laying off workers despite the increasing cost of living.

I spoke in Cleveland, Toledo, Gary, and Chicago. I came back feeling no happier than when I left. Nor did my next task make me feel any better. I worked for a while with the Communist Youth who were just starting a campaign in favor of universal military training. This campaign troubled me for it did not seem to fit in with the Teheran perspective for a long-term peace, nor with the happy optimism that was promoted when the Nazi armies were broken and peace seemed near.

The campaign for universal military training, the no-strike postwar pledge which the Communists were ballyhooing, and the labor-management charter were all straws in the wind and pointed to one thing: ultimate state control of the people.

When the Yalta conference had ended, the Communists prepared to support the United Nations Charter which was to be adopted at the San Francisco conference to be held in May and June, 1945. For this I organized a corps of speakers and we took to the street corners and held open-air meetings in the millinery and clothing sections of New York where thousands of people congregate at the lunch hour. We spoke of the need for world unity and in support of the Yalta decisions. Yet at the same time the youth division of the Communists was circulating petitions for universal military training.

The two seemed contradictory. But Communists do not cross wires in careless fashion. The truth was that the two campaigns were geared to different purposes: the need to control the people in the postwar period, and the need to build a world-wide machine to preserve peace. Since the communist leaders were evidently not envisioning a peace mechanism without armies, the obvious question then was: for whom and to what end were the Communists urging the building of a permanent army? Did they not trust their own peace propaganda?

CHAPTER THIRTEEN

By April, 1945, there was evidence of trouble in the Communist Party. Uneasiness increased among its functionaries. I first became aware of this in my work with the Italian Commission of the American Communist Party.

One day two foreigners appeared in our midst, recently come from Italy. Berti and Donnini were a smooth, attractive pair, who called themselves professors and had become leaders of the Italian Commission. They immediately started a controversy about the work among national minorities.

Earl Browder at the convention of 1944 had insisted on the elimination of a sense of difference among the foreign-born and had moved to have them treated as part of the American labor movement. To this Professors Berti and Donnini offered strenuous objections. They emphasized the importance of separate national organizations, of encouraging the foreign-born to use their languages, and of circulating foreign-language newspapers. They encouraged the organizing of the different national groups almost as if these were foreign colonies. It would strengthen the sense of nationalism among them, they asserted, a necessary thing for the building of world communism.

These two Party functionaries found themselves on the carpet for their unwelcome views. Plans were on foot to expel them. Then, suddenly, came the amazing news that they were members of the Italian Communist Party! Up to this point, like others, I had regarded them as honest but misguided foreigners with a penchant for disputation.

Now I realized that nothing they said had been unpremeditated, and that they were not speaking for themselves. They represented the International Communist movement and it was clear that Browder's approach to the national problem was in disfavor with some sections of world communism.

During a bitter meeting I learned that these two men were responsible for translating and giving to the Scripps-Howard press a letter by Jacques Duclos, published previously in a communist magazine, *Cahiers du communisme*, in France. This letter was to change the whole course of the communist movement in this country.

The letter, which appeared in the *World-Telegram* in May, 1945, ridiculed the Browder line of unity, his Teheran policy, and charged the American Communists with having betrayed the principles of Marx and Lenin. It called upon the American Communists to clean house, and literally demanded that they get back to the job of making a revolution. It branded Browder as a crass "revisionist" of Marxism-Leninism, and it called for his removal from office.

Immediate confusion and hysteria permeated the Party. Ninety per cent of the membership did not know who

Jacques Duclos was, nor did they understand what "revisionist" meant. No attempt was made to enlighten them. More important things were happening.

For one thing, a palace revolution was taking place at Twelfth Street, with William Z. Foster leading the forces of Marxist fundamentalism. The large corps of jobholders in the Party added to the confusion, for like horses in a burning stable they had lost all sense of discretion. Frightened at being caught in a state of "revisionism," even if they did not know what it meant, and feeling that the voice from overseas presaged a change in the line of world communism, they tried frantically to purge themselves of the error they did not understand but which they had evidently committed. They confessed in private and in public meetings that they had been remiss in their duty, that they had betrayed the workers by support of a program of class collaboration. There were some demonstrations of public self-flagellation that stirred in me feelings of disgust and pity.

It was a bewildering time. To me nothing made sense. Over and over I heard people say they had betrayed the workers. I saw members of the National Board look distraught and disclaim responsibility, plead they had not known what was going on, or that they had been afraid to speak up when they saw errors. They cried that Browder had confused and terrorized them. It was distressing to watch these leaders, who were at best ignorant of what had gone on or were at worst cowards.

Gil Green went about white-faced and distraught because he had been so closely identified with the chief — had, in fact, been known as Browder's boy. He, too, quickly disavowed all he had said about imperialism having come to an end. In fact, it was clear that we were now to believe again that imperialism was the last stage of capitalism, that it would inevitably lead to war and the communist revolution, and that the United States was the worst offender. Again we were to despise our own country as an exploiter of the workers.

Gil and Israel Amter asked me to write a public statement to be published in the *Daily Worker* in which I was to repudiate the recent policy and confess my errors. I tried, but my pen would not write the words. I excused myself by saying, "I don't understand what has happened. We don't seem to have all the facts." For I remembered how, as recently as the previous May, members of the Communist International had been present at the Party convention and had approved the line. And I remembered, too, that it was William Z. Foster who nominated Browder as president of the Communist Political Association. It was Foster who seconded the motion to dissolve the Party in 1944.

This was certainly a turn-about-face, a complete repudiation of a policy which had not only the unanimous support of the communist leadership in the United States, but the open support of the Soviet Union. We had even been told that the Teheran policy had been prepared with the assistance of Ambassador Oumansky, the accredited representative from the USSR to the United States.

Today it is obvious that after Stalin had gained diplomatic concessions at Yalta, and after the Bretton Woods and Dumbarton Oaks conferences had placed concealed American Communists in positions of power, world communism did not want the patriotic efforts of Earl Browder and his band of open Communists who longed for participation in American affairs. Only later did I learn that Foster's belated, polite, and restrained opposition to the Teheran line the year before had been suggested through private channels from abroad, as preparation for the upheaval of 1945.

Browder obviously was caught offguard and unprepared.

183

He was now compelled officially to present the Duclos letter to the membership for "discussion" through the columns of the *Daily Worker*. At meetings of the Party there was a wave of confused discussion, and the culmination of it was the calling of an emergency convention in June, 1945.

Much was to happen before that took place. The National Committee, almost sixty in number, was called into session at Twelfth Street to prepare for the convention. At first Irving Potash of the Furriers Union took the chair. Later Foster occupied it.

Browder was in the room. He had been ill and his appearance was that of a man in pain. Person after person studiously avoided speaking to him, and when he sat down he was entirely alone. Yet a hundred times I had seen these same people jump up when he came into a room and sing, "Browder is our leader. We shall not be moved." Now, when they looked at him, their faces were grim with hate, or perhaps it was fear.

I did not know Browder well. I was one of the newest members of the National Committee, but suddenly I could not bear this any longer. I arose from my seat at the opposite end of the room and walked over to Browder's chair and shook hands with him. Then I sat down in the empty chair next to his, though I was aware my action would not go unnoticed. I urged him to offer some explanation or at least to stay and meet the charges to be brought. But he said he could not stay for the meeting.

"I will not defend myself," he said firmly. "This is left-wing sectarian nonsense. They will come back."

I knew little about high politics within the communist apparatus, and I could not understand the upheaval nor why he gave up so easily. Even then I did not believe, as he evidently did, that there would be any return. Later,

184

when he went to the Soviet Union, I realized that he had gone to Moscow in the hope of reversing the decision.

The old National Committee met for three days. The meetings began early and lasted late. I looked for signs of understanding and kindness and compassion. I thought to find them at least among the women, but they were not there either. I thought that at least Mother Bloor, the so-called "sweetheart" of the movement, would counsel moderation, for she had been close to Browder. Instead, this old woman talked angrily about how stubborn Browder was and how "arrogant."

Elizabeth Gurly Flynn, formerly of the IWW, whom Browder had taken into the Party in 1938 and elevated to the National Committee, was not far behind Mother Bloor in her remarks. I could hardly believe my ears when I heard her state coldly that she had been intimidated by Browder, that she had been unaware of the fact that he was "liquidating" the Party, that she was out of headquarters so much that she had no knowledge of what was going on. I heard Ann Burlak, once known as the "Red Flame of New England," whom years as an organizer for the Party had reduced to a pallid, thin-lipped, silent creature, speak up and join the accusing pack.

I, myself, was neither for nor against Browder. Yet I almost got in trouble by replying to Ben Davis when he made a particularly cruel speech. Ben Davis was a Negro, a member of the New York City Council, and the previous year he had joined a Tammany Hall Democratic Club in order, he said, to get support for his next campaign for the City Council. Now he excoriated Browder for his "betrayal" of the Negro people in disbanding the Communist Party in the South. Browder had urged that the Party work in the South through broad front committees, such as the Southern Committee for Human Rights, because

185

he felt that the very name "Communist" shut all doors there.

I had seen this same Ben Davis use the united front line of collaboration in the crassest possible way to promote his own political ambitions and now I suddenly knew I must speak. I took the floor and asked where Ben Davis had been at the time when all this was being done. Surely anyone as sensitive as he to any betrayal of the Negro, I said, should have spoken up then and not have waited until now.

Ben Davis promptly turned his violence on me: I was guilty of chauvinism, he insinuated, since I expected him as a Negro to be sensitive to the problem of the Negro. This strange illogic left me wordless.

That same day several of the Negro members of the National Committee took me to lunch. Pettis Perry and William Patterson, both of whom I liked, tried to justify Ben Davis' intemperate attacks and said I did not understand the national minority question well. All I could think as I listened was, "Has everyone gone mad?"

Later that afternoon we heard more wailing and saw more breast-beating. When Pat Tuohy, an active Party organizer, formerly a Pennsylvania miner with memories of the Molly Maguires, got up to speak, I thought that now something sensible would be heard. Instead, Pat burst out crying, and said he had never agreed with the Teheran line, but that Browder had intimidated him by saying, "Pat, you're getting old. We can dispense with your services if you are in disagreement." Were these the men I had thought fearless fighters in the cause of justice?

Just before the National Committee closed its meeting it set up committees to prepare for the Emergency Convention. I was surprised to hear myself named to serve on a temporary committee of thirteen which was to interview all members of the National Board and National Committee, estimate the extent of their revisionist errors, and recommend to the National Convention those who should be dropped and those who should be retained for new leadership.

My work on that committee of thirteen was an experience I shall never forget. Bill Foster was technically chairman. His constant attendant was Robert Thompson. Davis of the Philadelphia A.F. of L. food workers' union and Ben Gold of the CIO Furriers were the ranking members. The procedure was fascinating and fantastic. It was the nearest thing to purge trials I have ever seen.

One by one the leaders appeared before this committee. We were silent and waited for them to speak. Men showed remorse for having offended or betrayed the working class. They tried desperately to prove that they themselves were of that working class, and had no bourgeois background, and were unspoiled by bourgeois education. They talked of Browder as if he were a sort of bourgeois Satan who had lured them into error because of lack of understanding due to their inadequate communist education. Now they grieved over their mistakes and unctuously pledged that they would study Marx-Lenin-Stalin faithfully, and never betray the working class again. One by one they came before the committee and I began to feel like one of Robespierre's committees in the French Revolution.

It was weird to see tall, rawboned Roy Hudson pick and choose his words with pathetic care, to hear him plead, as if it were a boast, that all he had was a third-grade education and that he came from a poverty-stricken background. It was weird to hear Thompson talk about his proletarian father and mother. It was strange to hear Elizabeth Gurly Flynn beg forgiveness and offer in extenuation that she was of Revolutionary stock, for her father had belonged to the R.A. in Ireland, then promise to study Marx and Lenin and to become a true daughter of the coming American revolution.

Sometimes an honest statement came, and it was a great relief. Such a one was when Pettis Perry said he had been an illiterate share cropper in the South and that the Party had helped him to learn to read and write and had given him the opportunity to discover what he could do.

As I listened to this insistence on poverty and lack of formal education as the qualifications for admission to this Party, I began to feel uneasy, and I turned to Alexander Trachtenberg, one of the thirteen on the committee.

"I don't think I belong here," I said. "It is true that my father and mother worked hard, but my father became a successful businessman and we owned a house and I went to college."

Trachtenberg, himself a well-educated man, caught the irony in my statement. He stroked his walrus mustache and said reassuringly: "Don't worry about that. Remember Stalin studied to be a priest and Lenin came from a well-to-do family and studied to be a lawyer. You must be a proletarian or identify yourself with the proletariat. That's all."

As the comrades continued to come before the examining committee the thought came to me that there was not one real worker among them. Foster, though he affected the khaki shirt of a workman, hadn't done a stroke of work in a long time. He had been sitting in little rooms planning revolutions and conniving for power for twenty-five years. Thompson and Gil Green had graduated from school right into the Young Communist League. Thompson had gone to Spain as a commissar of the Lincoln Brigade and when he returned he worked for the Party, and Gil became a Party functionary at an early age.

188

That was the pattern of these American revolutionaries, and I felt as I looked at them that they really could know little about the ordinary worker.

At the end of June the Emergency Convention met. Because of wartime travel restriction, Foster announced that there would be only a small number from the rest of the country. Some fifty delegates came. The New York delegates swamped the convention. The out-of-towners were window dressing. When Foster strode in with Thompson and Ben Davis at his heels I could think only of the victorious Fuehrer and his gauleiters.

The debate and the argument that went on at that convention I can only compare to conversation in a nightmare. One sensed threatening danger in the frenzied activity, but there was vagueness as to what it was all about, and as to where we were going. Confusion and universal suspicion reigned at the Fraternal Clubhouse on Forty-eighth Street which was the arena of the convention.

Close friends of many years' standing became deadly enemies overnight. Little cliques, based on the principle of mutual protection and advancement, sprang up everywhere. Some shouted slogans from Jacques Duclos. Some shouted down anyone who suggested logical discussion of problems. The mood, the emotions, were hysterically leftist with the most violent racist talk I ever heard.

Bill Lawrence, New York State secretary, who had fought in Spain, was attacked because of Browderism. He fended that off by asserting his loyalty to the Party. Then someone charged him with having been a coward in Spain, and I saw tears run down his face as he tried to explain to a group that wanted not explanations but executions. Ben Davis attacked Jim Ford, a Negro member of the National Board, and called him an "Uncle Tom," because he had been restrained in his attack on Browder.

189

The newly elected National Committee, which was elected on the third day, held its first meeting at 4 A.M. A new chairman and a secretary were still to be selected. Browder had appeared briefly at the Convention to address it. When this had first been suggested there were calls from the hall for his immediate hanging and loud cheers at the suggestion. However, he was allowed to speak, and he was most conciliatory, saying he approved the draft resolution and the establishing of a new line. He promised to co-operate.

When he finished, there was scattered applause in which I joined. I was sitting at a table with Israel Amter and I caught his beady black eyes fixed on me. Months later he brought me up on charges of having applauded Browder.

The Convention carried out various measures. It voted to dissolve the Communist Political Association and to re-establish the Communist Party. It voted to re-dedicate itself to its revolutionary task of establishing a Soviet America. It voted to intensify Marxist-Leninist education from the leaders down to the lowliest member. It voted to oust Browder as leader. It voted to return to the use of the word "comrade."

As for me, from that time on I became allergic to the use of that word, for I had seen many uncomradely acts at the Emergency Convention in the Fraternal Clubhouse.

CHAPTER FOURTEEN

THE NEW LINE established at the Emergency Convention was meant to be all things to all people. It was intended to be leftist enough to assuage those who had guilty feelings about betrayal of the working class, yet called for enough unity with so-called democratic forces to permit continued collaboration with the forces of "imperialism." Even so there were dissatisfied elements on both the right and the left.

At district conventions the new line was adopted with the hysteria that had characterized the National Convention. The same terror was apparent.

I was in a difficult spot. As legislative representative, I had to present to the New York District Convention the proposal for the selection of city-wide candidates for the November elections. A decision to support William O'Dwyer for mayor had been made by the state board before the Duclos bombshell. Now in the light of the changed line no one wanted to assume responsibility for supporting him.

It was obvious that the new leftist line would disrupt communist power in the field of practical politics, and yet the Party wanted to continue to control the balance of power in New York State politics. I was assigned to report to the Convention and to get a vote of approval for O'Dwyer.

The New York civil-service unions and the transport workers had been seething against LaGuardia for years. He had given them fair words but little or no wage increases. In 1941 the Party had considered supporting O'Dwyer but at the last moment had changed its mind and gone along with Hillman and Dubinsky in support of LaGuardia.

Now the die was cast, and we followed the election decisions made previously. With O'Dwyer's election the Communists placed one of their ablest men in City Hall as confidential secretary to the new mayor.

The new National Board had reshuffled Party posts. Gil Green was sent to Chicago in charge of the industrialized states of Illinois and Indiana. Robert Thompson was named by Eugene Dennis as leader of the New York district. When I heard of it my heart sank. In an unprecedented move I opposed his election on the ground that he had little experience in running so large and complex a district. He never forgave me for this slight to his vanity.

I tried to withdraw from my post as an employee of the Party but Thompson insisted on keeping me close at hand. I could not be silenced and we clashed repeatedly. I was uneasy and frightened, but I tried to believe that the madness which was on us was temporary. When Browder left for Moscow with a Soviet visa I hoped a change would come on his return. So I held on because I felt I had an obligation to do all in my power to get others to see how terrible were the things we planned to do. For, strange as it now seems to me, the last illusion to die in me was the illusion about the Soviet Union. I did not know then that the new line was made in Moscow.

The leadership of the Party in the United States might be wrong; the leadership of the French Party or of the Italian Party might be wrong; but faith in the socialist Motherland, in the Soviet Union, was deeply etched into our very being. The conditioning had been deep.

I ran into conflict after conflict with Thompson. He was Moscow-trained, morose, and unstable. He surrounded himself with strong-arm men and packed the state board meetings with those who flattered him and voted his way. He moved in swiftly to destroy anyone who thwarted him. He and Ben Davis tried to get me to prefer charges against Eugene Connolly, a city councilman and secretary of the American Labor Party, on the grounds of "white chauvinism." When I protested that I had never seen the slightest evidence of "white chauvinism," they looked at me in disgust.

They sought to move against Michael Quill on the ground that he had voted in favor of a city council resolution to greet Archbishop Spellman on his return from Rome as cardinal. At a tense meeting of the state board I protested this attempt against Quill and reminded Thompson that effective mass leaders who work with the Party are hard to find.

"Comrade Dodd forgets," said Thompson, "that communist leadership is superior to mass leadership. Anyone who opposes us must be eliminated from the labor movement."

I carried my appeal against such decisions to Eugene Dennis, but he only shrugged his shoulders and suggested I see the "old man." A talk with William Z. Foster made me decide never to seek him out again, so utterly cynical was his reply.

As 1945 dragged into the spring of 1946 it was clear that

Foster and Dennis had been ordered to take over the Party, but it was also clear that they did not know what to do with it. The depression in the United States predicted by a Soviet research group had not materialized and Foster and his aides, who were all poised for the revolutionary moment, were unable to agree on what to do. It became obvious there would be no Party convention in 1946.

In January of 1946 the National Board decided to expel Earl Browder from the Party, and he was brought up on charges by the little communist branch in Yonkers where he made his home. The charges were that he had advanced Keynesian ideas, that he maintained them stubbornly, and that he had been politically passive, and had failed to attend local club meetings.

He was tried by a handful of Yonkers Communists, but his expulsion was approved by the National Committee. The cruelty of such treatment for a past leader can be possible only in this strange movement, where there is no charity, no compassion, and, in the end, total elimination of those who have served it.

Late in 1945 word had come from Jessica Smith, wife of John Abt, who was in Moscow, that it was important that American women be organized into an international movement, ostensibly for peace. An international federation was to be established with Russian and French Party women as leaders. So during the next months I helped organize the United States branch. A combination of wealthy women and Party members established and maintained what was called the Congress of American Women.

Since it was supposedly a movement for peace, it attracted many women. But it was really only a renewed offensive to control American women, a matter of deep importance to the communist movement, for American women do 80 per cent of the family spending. In the upper brackets they own a preponderance of capital stock and bonds. They are important in the making of political decisions. Like youth and minority groups, they are regarded as a reserve force of the revolution because they are more easily moved by emotional appeals. So the Soviet campaign for peace was especially geared to gain support of the women.

From the day of the Emergency Convention there had been efforts to bring every Party member back into support of the new leadership. Some were won over with jobs. Others were given the public-humiliation treatment; some were permitted to hang around unassigned until their disaffection had cooled; and some were expelled.

From 1945 to 1947 several thousands were expelled, each individually with the refinement of terror in the purge technique. Two main reasons were given for expulsion: one was guilty either of leftism or rightism. Ruth McKenney, of *My Sister Eileen* fame, and her husband Bruce Minton, were among the first expelled, their crime being leftism.

A reign of terror began in which little people who had joined from idealistic notions were afraid the slightest criticism of the Party would bring the accusation of deviation. Some of these people appealed to me for help, for the Party's action endangered their reputations and jobs. I tried to help. I counseled restraint but I was often ineffective because I, myself, was in an equivocal position, something of which the Party was well aware. I had escaped punishment for my independence in 1945, possibly because I was not easy to deal with, for I had won for myself a position of respect with the rank-and-file members and had always remained close to my Union.

But a stealthy campaign had begun against me. Twice

that year I faced charges. My home and law office were invaded by Party investigators, who came in supposedly to chat and visit with me, and then reported at headquarters any unorthodox remark. My secretary was enlisted to report on who came to the office, on my relations with Party and non-Party members, and on the nature of my correspondence. A poor old seaman whom I fed and lodged while he was waiting for a job was naïve enough to tell me he was asked many questions about what was said and done at my home. I began to feel that if I frowned at a *Daily Worker* editorial someone would surely report it.

Twice they concocted a charge of white chauvinism against me. Once I was brought before Ray Hausborough, a Negro from Chicago, whom I liked and respected, and who heard the charges and dismissed them. Once I found myself before a woman's commission with Betty Gannet in the chair, again on a trumped-up charge dealing with chauvinism. I laughed at them for of all the white women present, I was the only one living in Harlem in friendship with my neighbors of all races.

All these charges were too slim to be sustained, but they concocted others. One accusation stemmed from the fact that I had blocked the Party's move to support one of their favorite union leaders who was facing charges of pilfering union funds. This charge was true, as I was shocked at the Party's support of such an unsavory character. This time I received such rough treatment from the comrades that when Thompson, who was in charge, leaned over the desk and started shouting at me, I stood up, knocked over the chair I had been sitting in, and said to them coldly: "You think like pigs," and slammed out of the room. But in my heart I was frightened at my own temerity.

The next day Bill Norman, the state secretary, who

served as a balance wheel to the explosive and unpredictable Thompson, called me to his office. He talked to me in his quiet and reasonable way and I told him frankly that I wanted to get out of the Party. His expression changed. He fixed his eyes on me and said, almost harshly, "Dodd, no one gets out of the Party. You die or you are thrown out. But no one gets out." Then he became his mild self again.

Finally I asked to have Si Gerson take my position as legislative representative and that I be assigned to the Marcantonio campaign that fall.

For the 1946 state elections, the Party had decided to place a communist ticket in the field to get a bargaining position in the American Labor Party apparatus which now consisted of the leaders of the Amalgamated Clothing Workers, Vito Marcantonio and his machine, and the Communists. A full slate of candidates was named and I was placed on it as candidate for attorney general, which of course I did not take seriously for I knew that the Party would later make deals with the American Labor Party and one of the two major parties, and then withdraw its own candidates.

The work of the 1946 elections was so masterfully contrived that the Communists, through the use of the American Labor Party and the unions they controlled, were successful in defeating all whom they seemed to be supporting. There was, however, one exception to this trickery and that was the campaign for the election of Representative Vito Marcantonio. For once the Republican Party had decided on a strong campaign against him. Marc was one of the ablest men in Congress, but he was also the recognized voice of the Communists. There were others in Congress who served them effectively. None was so capable or so daring in the promotion of Party objectives. I was happy to be put to work in the primary and election campaign in Marcantonio's district for it gave me a respite from the complications of Twelfth Street.

I was in charge of a difficult district, the upper Tenth, from Ninety-Sixth Street to 106th Street, and from the East River to Fifth Avenue. It was an unbelievably depressed area, the population largely Negroes recently from the South, Puerto Ricans lately from their island, and the remnants of Irish, Italian, Greek, and Jewish people, all living in one of the worst slums in New York.

There was only one oasis in the district, the new housing project on the East River. In this project lived a Republican captain named Scottoriggio who was an outspoken opponent of the Labor Party. This was unusual in this area, as that party usually had the co-operation of both Democratic and Republican leaders.

My headquarters were at Second Avenue and Ninety-ninth Street. My captains consisted of a group of teachers who were my friends, and Italian and Puerto Rican members of the Marcantonio machine, one of them Tony Lagana, a jobless young Italian with a deep devotion to Marcantonio.

In the registration campaign the teachers helped hundreds to pass the literacy tests. Many hours were spent helping these adults qualify for the right to vote. We practically doubled the registration figures. The election campaign was a bitter one with violence erupting everywhere. Among our leading opponents was Scottoriggio, who interfered with our campaign workers and challenged their effectiveness in canvassing the housing project. Hatred had reached a high pitch on the night before election day.

On election day I opened my headquarters at five o'clock in the morning. I served coffee and buns to my captains and then proceeded to make assignments. While we were drinking our coffee we listened to the radio on my desk, and heard the news that Scottoriggio, on his way to the polls, had been assaulted by four men and was in a hospital with a fractured skull.

We won the election. When Scottoriggio died of his injuries, the district was thrown into an uproar. The Republican leader and the police who had co-operated with Marcantonio for years were under fire. All my captains were called in for questioning, among them little Tony Lagana, who was taken to the 104th Street station and held for many hours. What happened there I do not know nor whom he implicated, nor how fast the information got to those he implicated. They finally let him go. That night he disappeared, and several months later his body was found in the East River.

I was subpoenaed by the New York County grand jury and interrogated at the district attorney's office. In the midst of the questioning one of the two assistants asked me why I had become a Communist.

"Because only the Communists seemed to care about what was happening to people in 1932 and 1933," I said. "They were fighting hunger and misery and fascism then, and neither the major political parties nor the churches seemed to care. That is why I am a Communist."

I spoke with the practiced intensity of long habit but no longer with the old faith in the cause, for I no longer had the same deep conviction about the Party's championship of the poor and dispossessed. I knew now that its activities were conceived in duplicity and ended in betrayal.

The sessions of the December National Committee were notable for their long-winded, long-spun-out, and fantastic justification of the line of "self-determination of the Negro in the black belt." Only the intelligence and patience of Negro leaders in America have made possible resistance to this mischievous theory which was contrived by Stalin and was now unleashed by Foster. Briefly told, it is the theory that the Negroes in the South form a nation, a subjugated nation with the desire to become a free one, and that the Communists are to give them all assistance. The Party proposed to develop the national aspirations of the Negro people so they would rise up and establish themselves as a nation with the right to secede from the United States. It was a theory not for the benefit of the Negroes but to spur strife, and to use the American Negro in the world communist propaganda campaign to win over the colored people of the world. Ultimately, the Communists proposed to use them as instruments in the revolution to come in the United States.

During those days I was ill in body and spirit. Mostly I stayed away from Twelfth Street and its meetings. When I did go I was aware of an extreme agitation among the Party bureaucrats. Factions were rising and in an atmosphere of increasing uncertainty and fear.

In the spring of 1947 Foster went to Europe, clearly to get instructions for action, and returned with the proud report that he had met Gottwald of Czechoslovakia, Dimitroff of Bulgaria, Togliatti of Italy, and Duclos of France. He also reported that he had been in England for the Empire meetings which brought the communist representatives of the various commonwealths to London.

No sooner had he returned than every sign of factionalism disappeared. A National Committee meeting was called for June 27, 1947. It continued for several days, and each day was filled with drama. It was clear to us gathered there that a reshuffling of leadership was near.

First of all, Morris Childs, editor of the *Daily Worker*, was removed from his office. Morris, who had recently returned from Moscow, had evidently done something to displease either Moscow or the Party in New York. He knew it himself, for no sooner had he returned than he asked for a six months' leave of absence, explaining he had heart trouble.

Eugene Dennis, national secretary of the Party, in making the organizational report, announced that Childs was to have an indefinite leave of absence, and then he proposed as the new editor a young man with the adopted name of John Gates. Childs's face turned white as a sheet, for neither he nor, as it turned out, the editorial board of the *Daily Worker* had been consulted about the new editor.

It was a strange choice. John Gates, a young veteran recently returned from overseas service, had no experience in newspaper work, but I did know that he had made contacts with powerful figures overseas, and on his return he had been placed in charge of veterans' work for the Party. There was a stir among the members about this selection. Foster put an end to dissent by saying flatly, "A communist leader does not need newspaper experience to be an editor. It is more important that he be a sound Marxist."

Following this statement, the vote was taken at once. It was unanimous in favor of Gates. There were two abstentions from approval — Morris Childs and myself. My vote was an overt act of rebellion against the steam roller which was being used on the National Committee. I knew that this meeting marked the end of my stay in the administration of the Party and so I decided to make the most of it. I knew there were others in the committee who felt as I did, but fear kept them from making the open break I now made.

I knew that no one in the Party ever attacks the persons in power chosen to give reports. They must be praised, and the report must be characterized as crystal clear and masterful. I knew, finally, that everyone was supposed to vote for it.

I decided to break with this tradition, first by my abstention in voting for Gates, and then by attacking Foster's next proposal: to postpone the Party convention until 1948. The constitution of the Party, which was proudly displayed every time the Party was attacked as undemocratic, provided for a regular convention every two years. The last had been held in 1944; the one in 1945 had been merely emergency. A convention was certainly due in 1947. I arose and said that we had no other choice but to live up to the constitution.

Some of the other members now spoke up and I saw the possibility of a tiny victory against the steam roller. Foster saw it, too, and in a voice of authority he said that, since all other political parties would be having conventions in 1948 for the nomination of candidates for president, the Communists ought to have theirs at the same time. He threw a withering glance at me and said, "Comrade Dodd's argument is legalistic," a remark which ended the discussion.

The report was voted on and approved.

The next item on the agenda was a political report on the coming elections of 1948 and the possibility of a third party. This report was given by John Gates, and the fact that he was chosen to give it showed that he was being groomed as a coming leader of the Party. Not only did he know nothing about running a newspaper, but he was relatively uninformed about American politics.

His report was obviously not his work. In fact, I could easily recognize it as the combined efforts of Eugene

202

Dennis and those Party members with whom he was in close touch through the American Labor Party, the Independent Committee of Artists, Scientists and Professionals, and the communist forces at Capitol Hill, especially the brilliant Albert Blumberg, once on the Johns Hopkins staff, whom I had first met at conventions of the American Federation of Teachers. I knew him as a regular courier between Dennis and the communist staff in Washington.

I listened carefully to the report, vague, contradictory, and full of words, repeating the old phrases about the need of a Labor Party in America. It did not state when it was to be built nor what were the special conditions which called for it at this particular time. The point of it all came near the end, when Gates read that a third party would be very effective in 1948, but only if we could get Henry Wallace to be its candidate.

There it was, plainly stated. The Communists were proposing a third party, a farmer-labor party, as a political maneuver for the 1948 elections. They were even picking its candidate.

When Gates had finished, I took the floor. I said that while I would not rule out the possibility of building a farmer-labor party, surely the decision to place a third party in 1948 should be based not on whether Henry Wallace would run, but on whether a third party would help meet the needs of workers and farmers in America. And if a third party were to participate in the 1948 elections, the decision should be made immediately by bona-fide labor and farmer groups, and not delayed until some secret and unknown persons made the decision.

My remarks were heard in icy silence. When I had finished, the committee with no answer to my objection simply went on to other work.

However, it was becoming evident that the top clique

was having a hard time about this proposition. It was also clear that Dennis and his crew of smart boys were reserving to themselves the right to make the final decision, and that the Party in general was being kept pretty much in the dark.

When the Progressive Party was finally launched it represented not the farmers and workers of America but the same kind of synthetic coalition which had become a pattern of communist participation in national politics. There were large numbers of disillusioned middle-class professionals in it; there were women of wealth, moved by humanitarian motives; and there were Communists and fellow travelers. All these elements were welded together by flashy professional publicity agents, glib of tongue and facile of pen.

The cynical attitude of the top Communists toward the Progressive Party can best be illustrated by its results. Early in January of 1948 and before Henry Wallace had made any public statement, in fact even before the Progressive Party had been formally organized, Foster announced through the Associated Press that it was going to be formed and that Henry Wallace would be its standard bearer.

Before election day it was clear that the Communists had perpetrated a fraud on those who were looking for a clear-cut party. For the Progressive Party, advertised as a farmer-labor party, was without the support of organized labor or of any basic farm organization. Aside from a few left-wing unions, labor support for it was synthetic.

On election eve I listened to Henry Wallace as he wound up his campaign on 116th Street and Lexington Avenue, in Marcantonio's district. He was only a second-string speaker to the congressman, and he seemed out of place there, far away from the cornfields of Iowa. He was the candidate of a farmer-labor party, and yet he was actually supported by neither. As a voice of protest he was so completely controlled by the Communists that Americans were repelled and the election results showed that he had received only a few more than 900,000 votes, of which the 600,000 were in New York State. He did not affect the national picture, though he did make a difference in New York State where he insured the victory for Thomas E. Dewey. He received fewer votes proportionately than did Eugene Debs when he ran on the socialist ticket after World War I while still in jail. La Follette in 1924 received four times as many votes.

The Communists had cleverly put Wallace forth as an inspirational leader and an idealist rather than a practical organizer. They had surrounded him with Foster's boys and the result was inevitable. Foster and Dennis became the leaders of the Progressive Party; Wallace was only its voice.

I had not understood why Foster should be dictating such apparently self-defeating policies to the Progressive Party. Now it was apparent that the reason they wanted a small limited Progressive Party was because it was the only kind they could control. They wanted to control it because they wanted a political substitute for the Communist Party, which they expected would soon be made illegal. A limited and controlled Progressive Party would be a cover organization and a substitute for the Communist Party if the latter were outlawed.

Also it was clear why at the National Committee meeting of June, 1947, Foster gave a report on underground organizations in Europe, in countries where the Communist Party faced illegality. He said that only the hard core would remain organized and all others would be reached through their trade unions and other mass organizations.

205

About 10 per cent of the Party would be organized in tight little groups of three — trade-union representatives, political representatives, and unorganized representatives. This was to be the underground party of illegality.

In fine, one could see that shuffling of personnel at the meeting had been carefully planned. It had squeezed out all those who had been put in for window dressing at the Duclos convention of 1945. Now the stalwarts and professionals of revolution took their appointed places and prepared to strike.

CHAPTER FIFTEEN

DURING the latter months of 1947 my world was shifting all about me. The certitude which I had so long known in the Communist Party was now gone. I was ill in mind and often in body, too, for I had a constant and terrible fear that every effort was being made to destroy me. I had watched the pitiless and methodical destruction of others. I did not have the will to fight back, nor did I want to involve the innocent.

At that period little dissident groups were forming and they criticized the Party, both from the right and the left. Each had its own leader. Each vowed devotion to the Party and each charged that the leadership of the Party in the United States had gone off the Marxist-Leninist track. I had noted the futility of such attempts before and, although I never refused to see anyone who sought me, I did refuse to become involved with them. I knew well that no group could be organized without being under the surveillance of Chester, the smooth, dapper director of the Party's secret service. His men were everywhere.

I turned to my law practice and sought to forget my fears by immersing myself in work, but inwardly I was so disturbed that my work suffered. I did not know how and when the ax would fall. I knew my office was still under constant surveillance and I had no way of stopping it. Certain agents from communist headquarters made a practice of visiting me at regular intervals trying to get me to take part in some meaningless activity. I knew well that was not the reason they came.

I remember particularly an Italian Communist whom Foster sent to me to discuss the raising of money for the 1948 elections in Italy. I felt the purpose was to enmesh me, and I said as much to the young Italian. Also I protested that raising money was not my specialty, and that the national office had only to lift the telephone to collect the fifty thousand dollars which I was asked to raise.

I was still accustomed, however, to obeying directions from the Ninth Floor. Instead of getting rid of my visitor, I found myself handed a list of people to call on, and together we visited various men of wealth who worked with the Party.

I had paid relatively little attention to this phase of communist activity while engaged in union and political work. The finances of the Party were never discussed at state or national committee meetings. No financial reports were given. Periodically we planned drives to raise money usually by asking a day's or a week's wages from workers.

Of course I knew that the Party had other sources of income but we never discussed them. I knew that they collected from a score of camps, and the reason I knew this was due to a hilarious incident after the war when Chester came to a secretariat board meeting to tell us he had a chance to buy a brand-new car for the Party's use at black-market prices. The board approved and then Chester an-

nounced that the car must of course be at his disposal because it was he who made the weekly rounds of the camps
to collect the money.

A bitter quarrel arose in which I was only a spectator.
Thompson, whose family was summering on Cape Cod,
felt he ought to have the new car since he was state chairman. Bill Norman, always the compromiser, proposed that
it go to Thompson, and that Thompson's car go to him,
Bill, since he was secretary, and that Bill's go to Chester.
I do not now remember who got the new car, but I do
remember that Chester collected considerable money from
the summer camps, both Youth and Adult.

During the war I became aware that the Party had an
interest in a certain machine plant engaged in war con-
tracts and that it drew revenue from it. I had long known
that the Party had an interest in printing and lithograph
plants, and in stationery and office supplies — shops where
all the unions and mass organizations directed their business through office managers who were Party members.

Several night clubs were started with the assistance of
wealthy political figures snagged by some of the most
attractive communist "cheesecake" in the Party. I used to
sympathize with these pretty Communists when some of
them rebelled because they said they were not being given
sufficient Marxist education. Instead, their time went into
calling on men and women of wealth, in an effort to get
them to open their pocketbooks. These girls, nearly all of
them college graduates, and some of them writers for the
slick magazines, were mostly from out of town and still
had a fresh-faced look and an innocent charm.

I noted that after a while they forgot their eager desire
for more Marxist education and developed a keen competition for private lists of suckers and private telephone numbers. These young women were capable of raising fabulous

sums. It was they who raised the first money for the night clubs which had been called Bill Browder's Folly, Bill being Earl's brother. But these night clubs paid off in money and in political prestige. They were also the means of attracting scores of talented young people who got their first chance to perform, and at the same time had the excitement of knowing they were part of a secret movement of revolt.

The Party boys who had worked on congressional committees, like the Truman committee which investigated the condition of the small businessman, had made valuable contacts for the Party's participation in the business world. It was they who steered the establishment of the Progressive Businessmen's Committee for the election of Roosevelt. Through them the Party had entree into local chambers of commerce and conservative business organizations like the Committee on Economic Development, in which Roy Hudson's wife held an important research job. Party economic researchers, accountants, and lawyers got jobs with various conservative planning groups in Republican and Democratic Party setups and in nonpartisan organizations.

The director of much of this activity was William Wiener, head of Century Publishers, who was known as the top financial agent of the communist movement, and who also operated a large financial empire. He was a mild, pudgy little man, who wore Brooks Brothers suits, smoked expensive cigars, and frequented expensive restaurants. The average Party member had no contact with men like him, for a functionary who earned an average of fifty dollars a week seldom saw this side of the Party.

Wiener had a number of financial pools operating to gather in capital from wealthy, middle-class Party people. They maintained offices with scores of accountants and at-

torneys from whom the communist movement drew re-
serves. There were doll factories, several paint and plastic-
manufacturing firms, chemical firms, tourist travel bureaus,
import-export companies, textiles and cosmetics, records
for young people, and theatrical agencies. In 1945 several
corporations were established for trade with China in one
of which was Frederick V. Field. Under the direction of
Wiener and others, such corporations hired and maintained a different type of communist, better-dressed,
better-fed, more sophisticated, and much more venomous.

The export-import group was especially interesting. I
recall one group of communist operators who brought
watch parts from Switzerland, assembled them here, and
sent the finished product to Argentina. I met one man who
was making regular flying trips to Czechoslovakia,
engaged in the deadly business of selling arms and ammunition, for today the communist agent engaged in
international trade is far more effective than the old-type
political agitator.

Now, as I traveled about the city trying to help raise
money for the Italian elections, I realized more than ever
how many major financial operations were touched by the
Party. In one office we visited a Party concern that bought
pig iron in Minnesota and shipped it to northern Italy
where, with the help of Italian Communist Party leaders,
it was allocated to communist-led plants and there proc-
essed into steel and shipped to Argentina. In another
office were lawyers who were deeply involved in the business of making money as custodians of alien property —
that of Italian citizens which had been seized during the
war. Assignments like these were not easy to get, but these
men got them.

After I had introduced my young Italian associate to a
number of people who professed themselves willing to

help, he decided to establish a permanent committee in the United States for cultural ties with Italy. Thus was born the American Committee for Cultural Relations with Italy. John Crane, whose family fortune was made in bathroom fixtures, was made chairman.

It was not that I had not known that the Communist Party used the rich as well as the worker, but I had never seen it so clearly before.

That spring I worked at my law practice and tried to build a private life for myself. I outwitted a number of well-laid plans to injure me. I learned during those months that some of the agents of the International Communist movement look and talk like your next-door neighbor. While I still saw many rank-and-file Communists, I avoided contact with the rest when I could.

Each morning when I woke to face another difficult day I would say to myself: "How did I get into this blind alley?"

I hoped against hope that I would be permitted to drift away from the Party. After all, a million and more Americans had drifted into and out of it. But I knew they were not likely to allow anyone who had reached a position of importance to do so.

I had withdrawn from most activity with them, except that I continued as Party contact for the Party teachers' groups. Now I was replaced even there and by a man who knew nothing at all about education. I was not attending Party meetings. Nevertheless, when I received a notice I decided to go to the state convention held that year in Webster Hall on the East Side.

There I found I was a marked person, that people were afraid to be seen sitting with me. After some hesitation, I finally sat down at a table beside David Goldway. He and

I had always been friends, and I knew he was having trouble as secretary of the Jefferson School. He greeted me only with his eyes and with a short nod of the head. His lips were a thin line. He did not smile or speak.

I heard loud voices at the entrance door and Thompson strode in, Ben Davis strutting at his heels, followed by a troop of young people. Suddenly I was reminded of my visit to Germany in the thirties when in Munich I had seen that same intense look on young faces devoted to Hitler, their leader.

When a state delegation to the coming National Convention was nominated by the presidium, I was amazed to hear some brave soul nominating me from the floor. I recognized him as a man from the Italian Commission. There was no purpose in my refusing, for I knew my name would not be presented for a vote. I was right. The presidium struck my name out with no explanation.

When the convention closed, the floor was cleared to set up tables for dinner. I left, for I knew I could not break bread with them.

As a member of the National Committee I had an obligation to attend the National Convention of 1948, but I decided I had punished myself enough. There was no reason for me to go; there was nothing I could do. Perhaps when that was over, when I was no longer a member of the National Committee, they would drop me entirely.

Evidently some of the leaders had thought I might go to the convention and had planned a means to silence me. Just before the convention the discipline committee ordered me to appear before it on the ninth floor.

I knew perfectly well that I did not have to obey this command. I was an American citizen with the right to be free of coercion. I did not have to go to Twelfth Street and ride the dingy elevator to the ninth floor. I did not

213

have to face the tight-lipped faces of the men and women who kept the gates and doors locked against intrusion, nor meet their eyes, scornful now because they knew I was *persona non grata*. I did not have to go, but like an automaton I went.

When I left the elevator I went through the long, dark corridor into an untidy room. Suddenly I all but laughed with relief, for there sat three old men — and I knew them all well. Alexander Trachtenberg, with his little walrus mustache and his way of looking down his nose, said nothing as I came in. Pop Mindel, the hero of the communist training schools, whose bright brown eyes were usually merry, had no smile for me. The third was Jim Ford, a Negro leader, whose look at me was distant and morose.

I greeted them and sat down. "At least," I said to myself, "these are men who know the score." My relationship with all of them had been friendly and we had never had any disputes. Now I waited for them to speak, but they sat there in silence until finally I grew uneasy. "Will this take long?" I asked Trachtenberg. With that he cleared his throat and spoke, and I could hardly believe what he was saying.

"How are you feeling?" he asked with no concern whatever in his voice.

I hedged. "I've been ill, Comrade Trachtenberg."

"But you are all right now?"

"Yes," I said. "I guess I'm all right now."

When he spoke again his German accent was stronger than usual. "We want to ask you a few questions."

"Here it comes," I thought, and braced myself. And then I found myself saying inwardly, "Dear God, dear God," with such an intensity that it seemed I had spoken aloud.

"We hear you attacked the Cominform," said Trachten-

214

berg, half-asking, half-accusing me. Then he stated the time and place where I had done it.

This I could answer. I explained carefully that I had criticized the *Daily Worker* statement which said the reason the Communist Party in America had not joined the Cominform was that it would be dangerous to do so. I had pointed out that this was a false statement and that no one would believe it.

They listened to my brief explanation. They did not say yea or nay to it. Pop Mindel's eyes got smaller and his lips more tightly compressed. There was another interval of silence, then Trachtenberg said, "We hear you do not like Thompson."

"Really, Comrade Trachtenberg, whether I like Thompson or not has nothing to do with the case," I said. Nevertheless I went on to explain my own feeling about him: that he was a menace to the lives of the American workers, and that he endangered the safety of our members.

The next question was unexpected.

"Were you born a Catholic?"

I rallied. "Yes," I said, wondering why this was asked. I could think of only one reason: my fight with Thompson over the Sharkey resolution relating to the greeting of Cardinal Spellman several years ago. I looked at the three shrewd men, so wise in the ways of communist planning, and could find no clue to the real reason. They knew well I had been born a Catholic; they knew I had followed no religion for many years. Then why the question?

They did not continue the inquiry. Suddenly Trachtenberg asked me why I was not active any longer in membership, why my activity was at a standstill.

I hedged. "I am still not quite well, Comrade Trachtenberg. And I have personal problems. Let me alone until I can find myself again."

215

There was another long silence. "Shall I go?" I asked at last, but received no direct answer.

"You will hear from us again," said Trachtenberg.

I was dismissed, and I walked out of the room, still wondering about this strange interrogation that had no beginning and no end. No doubt it was to keep me from going to the convention because they were afraid I might make embarrassing statements which would leak to the press. They need not have feared. I was in no condition to take the initiative in anything so difficult.

A new plan against me developed in the following weeks, a strategy of slurs, character defamation, harassments. There were, of course, still many people in the trade-union movement and especially teachers who were not part of the inner communist circle who remembered the days of my campaigning. Now the Party decided to blacken my character publicly so that the simple working people in the Party who liked me would no longer have confidence in me.

The incident which was used as the excuse for my formal expulsion from the Party was of no importance in itself. The way in which it was handled was symptomatic of Party methods. On Lexington Avenue, a few doors from my home, lived a Czechoslovakian woman with whom I sometimes talked. She lived in a small three-story building where she served as janitor from 1941 to 1947. Her husband was permanently incapacitated and she was the sole support of the family. Acting as a janitor and working as a domestic several days a week, she managed to keep her family together.

In 1947 the owner of the building decided to sell it. The woman, afraid she would lose both her apartment and her job, made up her mind to buy it, and borrowed the money to do so. Thus she became technically a landlord; but her daily life remained the same; she was still the janitor. However, as owner of the house she had become involved with her tenants and in quick succession three judgments were entered against her. Her husband quarreled and left her. The attorney for the plaintiffs, eager to collect his fees, asked warrants for her arrest.

At this point she came to me for help and I agreed to represent her. In the end the court granted my plea, the tenants were paid, and the woman escaped imprisonment.

One thing was clear: only technically could she have been called a landlord. But the communist leadership heard with delight that Bella Dodd had appeared as "attorney for a landlord." At last they had the excuse for getting me politically, the excuse for which they had been looking. Of course they could have simply expelled me but this would involve discussion of policies. They were looking for an excuse to expel me on charges that would besmirch my character, drive my friends away, and stop discussion instead of starting it. What better than to expel me for the crime of becoming a "hireling of the landlords"?

They must have realized that such an argument would scarcely be cogent to outsiders. Even to many of the Party it was weak. They must add something really unforgivable to make me an outcast in the eyes of the simple people of the Party. They did this by spreading the story that in my court appearances I had made remarks against the Puerto Rican tenants, that I had slandered them, and showed myself a racist, almost a fascist. And last of all, a charge of anti-Negro, anti-Semitism, and anti-working class was thrown in for good measure.

On May 6 a youth leader of the Communist Party, a round-faced, solemn youth, came to my house. I asked him in and offered him a cup of coffee, which he refused. Instead, he handed me a copy of written charges. When I said something about their falseness after I glanced through them, he gave me a sneering look and instructed me to appear for trial the next day at the local section commission, a block from my house.

I climbed the endless stairs to the drab, dirty meeting room with its smell of stale cigarettes. A group was waiting for me and I saw it consisted entirely of petty employees of the Party, those at the lowest rung of the bureaucracy. The three women among them had faces hard and full of hate — Party faces, I thought, humorless and rigid. They sat there like fates ready to pass on the destinies of human beings.

I had no quarrel with these people. In fact, as I looked at the group I had the feeling of a schoolteacher when small children become suddenly defiant of authority. One woman, the chairman, was Finnish. Another, a Puerto Rican, began shouting her hatred of me. At least it must have been hate to judge from her expression, for her English was too hysterical to be understood. The pudgy-faced boy was there, too. Of the other three men I recognized one as a waiter and the other as a piccolo player whom I had befriended.

This was an odd kind of trial. The Commission before me had already made up its mind. I asked whether I could produce witnesses. The answer was "No." I asked if I might bring the woman involved in the case to let her state the story. The answer was "No." I asked if the Commission would come with me to her house and speak with her and the tenants. The answer was "No." Then I asked if I might bring a communist lawyer who at least understood the legal technicalities I had been faced with in trying this simple case. The answer was "No."

As simply as possible I tried to explain the facts to them. From the start I realized I was talking to people who had been instructed, who were hostile, and would continue so despite arguments or even proof. The Finnish woman who was chairman said that I would be informed of the result.

I was dismissed. As I walked down the dingy steps my heart was heavy. The futility of my life overcame me. For twenty years I had worked with this Party, and now at the end I found myself with only a few shabby men and women, inconsequential Party functionaries, drained of all mercy, with no humanity in their eyes, with no good will of the kind that works justice. Had they been armed I know they would have pulled the trigger against me.

I thought of the others who had been through this and of those who were still to go through this type of terror. I shivered at the thought of harsh, dehumanized people like these, filled with only the emotion of hate, robots of a system which was heralded as a new world. And I sorrowed for those who would be taken down the long road whose end I saw, now, was a dead end.

When I reached my own house and went in, the rooms were cool and quiet. I was tired and spent, as if I had returned from a long, nightmare journey.

Of course I was certain more trouble was in store for me. This step had been merely preliminary to publicity against me, clever publicity. For this expulsion had not originated in the dirty rooms of the Harlem Commission, but from the headquarters on Twelfth Street, and perhaps from more distant headquarters.

I dreaded the coming publicity and decided to get in touch with the one group whom I had regarded as my friends. I called the Teachers Union to tell the Party leaders what was surely coming. I thought they would understand and discount any false accusations.

I need not have bothered. From the testimony of John

Lautner months later before the Senate Internal Security Committee I learned that Rose Russell and Abraham Lederman, leaders of the Teachers Union, had been present at the State Party meeting which engineered and confirmed my expulsion and issued the resolution to the press. The vote had been unanimous.

On June 17, 1949, my telephone rang. "This is the Associated Press," said a voice. "We have received a statement from the Communist Party announcing your expulsion from membership. It says here that you are anti-Negro, anti-Puerto Rican, anti-Semitic, anti-labor, and the defender of a landlord. Have you any statement to make?"

What statement could I make? "No comment," was all I could manage to say.

The New York papers carried the story the following day and three days later the *Daily Worker* reprinted the long resolution of expulsion, signed by Robert Thompson.

CHAPTER SIXTEEN

To THE New York newspapers the story of the expulsion of a woman Communist was merely one more story. It was handled in the routine way. I winced, however, when reputable papers headlined the Communist Party charges and used the words "fascism" and "racism," even though I knew these words were only quoted from the Party resolution.

I braced myself for further attacks from the Party, and they came soon in terms of economic threats. Some of my law practice came from trade-union and Party members, and here action was swift. The union Communists told me there would be no more referrals to me. Party members who were my clients came to my office, some with their new lawyers, to withdraw their pending cases.

Reprisals came, too, in the form of telephone calls, letters, and telegrams of hate and vituperation, many of them from people I did not know. What made me feel desolate were the reprisals from those I had known best, those among the teachers whom I had considered friends. While I was busy with Party work I sometimes thought proudly of my hundreds of friends and how strong were the ties that bound us. Now those bonds were ropes of sand.

What I had failed to understand was that the security I felt in the Party was that of a group and that affection in that strange communist world is never a personal emotion. You were loved or hated on the basis of group acceptance, and emotions were stirred or dulled by propaganda. That propaganda was made by the powerful people at the top. That is why ordinary Communists get along well with their groups: they think and feel together and work toward a common goal.

Even personal friends, some of whom I myself had taken into the Party, were lost to me now, and among them were many of my former students and fellow teachers. If rejection by an individual can cause the emotional destruction which our psychiatrists indicate, it cannot, in some ways, compare with the devastation produced by a group rejection. This, as I learned, is annihilating.

In vain I told myself that this was a big world and that there were many people other than Communists in it. It brought no consolation, for the world was a jungle in which I was lost, in which I felt hunted. Worst of all, I felt a constant compulsion to explain myself to those I met who were still in the communist circle. I tried at first, but soon gave it up.

I had always been an independent person and rarely gave my reasons for doing things. Now I wrote letters to people, some of whom had lived in my house or had been frequent guests there, and in whose homes I had been welcome. Those who replied were either abusive or obviously sought to disassociate themselves from me. Two friends replied in one sentence on the back of the letter I had written them only this: "Please do not involve us." Many did not answer at all.

Before long my office was empty except for snoopers and creditors. I gave up my home and moved into a dingy room near my office. I would go early to my office, read the *Times* and the *Law Journal,* and then sit and look out at Bryant Park, at the classical lines of the Public Library. I had spent many hours in that library as student and teacher, hungry for knowledge. Unfortunately I never really satisfied that hunger, for my reading in later years had been only communist literature and technical material. There is no censorship of reading so close and so comprehensive as that of the Party. I had often seen leaders pull books from shelves in homes and warn members to destroy them.

But I had no desire to read now. The one book I did open was the New Testament which I had never stopped reading even in my days of starkest Party delusion.

I stayed late in my office because there was no place to go other than my room, a dark, unpleasant place, with the odor of a second-class hotel. I still remember the misery and darkness of the first Christmas alone. I stayed in my room all day. I remember the New Year which followed, when I listened with utter despair to the gayety and noise from Times Square and the ringing bells of the churches. More than once I thought of leaving New York and losing myself in the anonymity of a strange town. But I did not go. Something in me struggled with the wave of nihilism engulfing me. Something stubborn in me told me I must see it through.

The New York *Post* asked me to write a series of articles on why I had broken with the Communist Party, and made me a generous offer. I agreed. But when I had finished them and read them over I did not want to see them published and found an excuse for refusing the offer. When a weekly magazine made an even more lucrative offer, I refused that, too. There were several reasons for this, as I now realize: one was that I did not trust my own conclusions, and another that I could not bear to hurt people I had known in the Party and for whom I still felt affection. Some I knew were entrapped as surely as I had been.

It was a strange and painful year. The process of completely freeing oneself emotionally from being a Communist is a thing no outsider can understand. The group thinking and group planning and the group life of the Party had been a part of me for so long that it was desperately difficult for me to be a person again. That is why I have lost track of whole days and weeks of that period.

But I had begun the process of "unbecoming" a Communist. It was a long and painful process, much like that of a polio victim who has to learn to walk all over again. I had to learn to think. I had to learn to love. I had to drain the hate and frenzy from my system. I had to dislodge the self and the pride that had made me arrogant, made me feel that I knew all the answers. I had to learn that I knew nothing. There were many stumbling blocks in this process.

One afternoon in March of that year an old acquaintance, Wellington Roe, came into my office. He breezed in with a broad smile and said he was just passing and had decided to say hello. I thought nothing further of his visit. "Duke," as we all called him, had been one of the Party's front candidates in the American Labor Party. He was the leader of the Staten Island forces and had run for office on its ticket. He had helped in the fight against Dubinsky when the Party was struggling to get complete control of the Labor Party. I had not known him as a Party member but as a liberal and a friend of the Party, one who did not mind being used for their campaigns.

It was reassuring to talk about the Party in terms of the average newspaperman, and laugh at its strange antics which he lampooned. I told him about my articles and he said he wanted to see them and even spoke of a possible book contract. Then he talked of events in Washington. I told him I had been so immersed in my own troubles that I had paid little attention to current events. If I had any opinion about Senator McCarthy, of whom he spoke, and of whom the country was just becoming aware, it was that I thought of him as the opening gun in the Republican campaign.

He asked if I had ever known Owen Lattimore. I said I had not. Had I ever known him to be a Party member, he asked, and again I said no. I had heard of him vaguely, I said, as a British agent in the Far East.

A few weeks later Duke walked in again and this time asked if I would be willing to help Professor Lattimore. I replied I did not see how, since I did not know him. He talked of the importance of having all liberals unite to fight reaction wherever it was manifesting itself. This left me unconvinced. I had problems of my own and for once I did not wish to get involved with those of others. But he came again the next day, this time with a man he introduced as Abe Fortas, Lattimore's attorney. I did not know him, but I had heard of him through mutual friends as a man who often defended civil-service employees faced with loyalty probes.

After a short talk the attorney said he thought he would have to subpoena me in the defense of Lattimore. When he saw my reluctance he asked if I would be willing to give him an affidavit saying that I had not heard of Lattimore while I was a leader in the Communist Party. So I

225

signed an affidavit to that effect, and I thought that was the end of it.

I was naïve to think so. A few days later I was served with a subpoena by the Foreign Relations Committee of the Senate. Dumfounded, I called Duke. He said it was no surprise to him. Since he was going to Washington he would be happy to make a reservation for me. He would even rent a typewriter so that I could prepare a statement.

At the hearings I saw Lattimore for the first time. Duke was there too. At a table with Senator Tydings sat Senator Green of Rhode Island, Senator McMahon of Connecticut, Senator Lodge of Massachusetts, and Senator Hickenlooper of Indiana. Back of them sat Senator McCarthy, and next to him Robert Morris, whom I had known as one of the attorneys for the Rapp-Coudert Committee.

I studied the senators before me. I knew that Senator Tydings was related in some way to Joseph Davies, former ambassador to Russia, who had written the friendly *Mission to Moscow,* and who had been active in Russian War Relief, receiving an award from the Soviet propaganda center in the United States, the Russian Institute. I knew of Senator McMahon's proposal for sharing our atomic knowledge with Russia. I felt that these men in the seats of power had facts not available to the rest of us, and were going along with the postwar perspective of co-existence with the Soviet Union, a position easy for me to accept since it was much like the communist propaganda during the years of my involvement with the communist world. When Senator Hickenlooper began to throw hostile questions at me I reacted with the hostility of the Communist, and I gave slick, superficial answers, for I did not want to be drawn into what I regarded as a Democratic-Republican fight.

There is no doubt in my mind that on *facts* of which I

had knowledge I told the truth. But when it came to questions of opinion there is no doubt that before the Tydings Committee I still reacted emotionally as a Communist and answered as a Communist. I had broken with the structure of the Party, but was still conditioned by the pattern of its thinking, and still hostile to its opponents.

Something, however, happened to me at this hearing. I was at last beginning to see how ignorant I had become, how long since I had read anything except Party literature. I thought of our bookshelves stripped of books questioned by the Party, how when a writer was expelled from the Party his books went, too. I thought of the systematic rewriting of Soviet history, the revaluation, and in some cases the blotting out of any mention of such persons as Trotsky. I thought of the successive purges. Suddenly I too wanted the answers to the questions Senator Hickenlooper was asking and I wanted the truth. I found myself hitting at the duplicity of the Communist Party.

I returned to New York alone and as the train sped through the darkness I looked out at the dim outline of houses in small towns and my heart went back to the memory of myself walking about the little Episcopalian cemetery as a child and putting flowers on the graves of American heroes. And suddenly I was aware of the reality of what was facing the country, a sobering fear of the forces planning against its way of life. I had an overwhelming desire to help keep safe from all danger all the people who lived in those little towns.

My appearance before the Tydings Committee had served one good purpose: it had renewed my interest in political events, and it had the effect of breaking the spell which had held me. I had at last spoken openly and critically of the Communist Party.

To those who find it difficult to understand how a mind

can be imprisoned, my puny indictment of the communist movement before the Tydings Committee may have seemed slight indeed, for I no doubt gave some comfort to the Party by my negative approach. But it takes time to "unbecome" a Communist.

But the event had been important to myself. I could now breathe again. I could read critically, and I lived again in the world so long lost to me.

I read the congressional report of the hearings on the Institute of Pacific Affairs. I found I was again able to interpret events. In my time with the Party I had accumulated a large store of information about people and events, and often these had not fitted into the picture presented by the Party to its members. It was as if I held a thousand pieces of a jigsaw puzzle and could not fit them together. It irritated me, but when I thought of the testimony of witnesses before the Congressional Committee, some of whom I had known as Communists, much of the true picture suddenly came into focus. My store of odd pieces was beginning to develop into a recognizable picture.

There had been many things I had not really understood. I had regarded the Communist Party as a poor man's party, and thought the presence of certain men of wealth within it accidental. I now saw this was no accident. I regarded the Party as a monolithic organization with the leadership in the National Committee and the National Board. Now I saw this was only a façade placed there by the movement to create the illusion of the poor man's party; it was in reality a device to control the "common man" they so raucously championed.

There were many parts of the puzzle which did not fit into the Party structure. Parallel organizations which I had dimly glimpsed now became more clearly visible, and their connections with the apparatus I knew became apparent. As the war in Korea developed, further illumination came to me.

We in the Party had been told in 1945, after the publication of the Duclos letter, that the Party in the United States would have a difficult role to play. Our country, we were told, would be the last to be taken by the Communists; the Party in the United States would often find itself in opposition not only to the interests of our government, but even against the interests of our own workers.

Now I realized that, with the best motives and a desire to serve the working people of my country, I, and thousands like me, had been led to a betrayal of these very people. I now saw that I had been poised on the side of those who sought the destruction of my own country.

I thought of an answer Pop Mindel, of the Party's Education Bureau, had once given me in reply to the question whether the Party would oppose the entry of our boys into the Army. I had asked this question at a time when the Communists were conducting a violent campaign for peace, and it seemed reasonable to me to draw pacifist conclusions. Pop Mindel sucked on his pipe and with a knowing look in his eyes said:

"Well, if we keep our members from the Army, then where will our boys learn to use weapons with which to seize power?"

I realized how the Soviets had utilized Spain as a preview of the revolution to come. Now other peoples had become expendable — the Koreans, North and South, the Chinese soldiers, and the American soldiers. I found myself praying, "God, help them all."

What now became clear to me was the collusion of these two forces: the Communists with their timetable for world control, and certain mercenary forces in the free world bent on making profit from blood. But I was alone with these thoughts and had no opportunity to talk over my conclusions with friends.

The year dragged on. Spring changed to summer and summer into autumn, days and problems were repeated in weary monotony. The few people I came in contact with were as displaced as myself. There were several, out of the Party like myself, who were struggling to find their way back to the world of reality. One was being psychoanalyzed and several were drinking themselves into numbed hopelessness.

More than once I wondered why I should go on living. I had no drive to make money. When I did make some, I paid creditors or gave it away. I paid the persons who pressed me hardest. Sometimes I went to visit members of my family, my brothers and their children. But from these visits I returned more desolate than ever. I had lost my family; there was no returning.

Every morning and every evening I walked along Sixth Avenue and Forty-second Street. I came to know the characters who congregated around there, the petty thieves, the pickpockets, the prostitutes, the small gamblers, and the sharp-faced, greedy little men. I, too, was one of the rejected.

Early in the fall of 1950 I went to Washington to argue an immigration appeal. I had planned to return to New York immediately afterward. It was a clear, crisp day, and I walked along Pennsylvania Avenue toward the Capitol. Near the House Office Building I ran into an old friend, Christopher McGrath, the congressional representative of the Twenty-seventh District, the old East Bronx area of my childhood. I had not seen him for more than a year. When I last saw him he had taken me to lunch and given me some advice. He greeted me warmly and invited me to his office. I was happy to go with him. There

I found Rose, his secretary, whom I had known. When we were in his private office he said abruptly: "You look harassed and disturbed, Bella. Isn't there something I can do for you?"

I felt a lump in my throat. I found myself telling him how much he had helped me the day he had taken me to lunch, and how good it had been to talk about my mother to someone who had known her.

I recalled how strange that luncheon visit had been. For the first time in many years and in a noisy restaurant in Manhattan someone had talked to me reverently about God. The people I had known in my adult life had sworn in the name of God or had repeated sophisticated jokes on religion, but none had talked of God as a living personal Reality.

He asked me if I wanted FBI protection, and I must have shivered noticeably. Though I was afraid, I was reluctant to live that kind of life. He did not press the issue. Instead, he said: "I know you are facing danger, but if you won't have that protection, I can only pray for your safety."

He looked at me for a moment as if he wanted to say something else. Then he asked: "Bella, would you like to see a priest?"

Startled by the question, I was amazed at the intensity with which I answered, "Yes, I would."

"Perhaps we can reach Monsignor Sheen at Catholic University," he said. Rose put in several calls and an appointment was made for me late that evening at the Monsignor's home.

I was silent as we drove to Chevy Chase. All the canards against the Catholic Church which I had heard and tolerated, which even by my silence I had approved, were threatening the tiny flame of longing for faith within me.

I thought of many things on that ride, of the word "fascist," used over and over by the communist press in describing the role of the Church in the Spanish Civil War. I also thought of the word "Inquisition" so skillfully used on all occasions. Other terms came to me — reactionary, totalitarian, dogmatic, old-fashioned. For years they had been used to engender fear and hatred in people like me.

A thousand fears assailed me. Would he insist that I talk to the FBI? Would he insist that I testify? Would he make me write articles? Would he see me at all? And then before my mind's eye flashed the cover of a communist pamphlet on which was a communist extending a hand to a Catholic worker. The pamphlet was a reprint of a speech by the French Communist leader Thorez and it flattered the workers by not attacking their religion. It skillfully undermined the hierarchy in the pattern of the usual communist attempt to drive a wedge between the Catholic and his priest.

By what right, I thought, was I seeking the help of someone I had helped revile, even if only by my silence? How dared I come to a representative of that hierarchy?

The screeching of the brakes brought me back to reality. We had arrived, and my friend was wishing me luck as I got out of the car. I rang the doorbell and was ushered into a small room. While I waited, the struggle within me began again. Had there been an easy exit I would have run out, but in the midst of my turmoil Monsignor Fulton Sheen walked into the room, his silver cross gleaming, a warm smile in his eyes.

He held out his hand as he crossed the room. "Doctor, I'm glad you've come," he said. His voice and his eyes had a welcome which I had not expected, and it caught me unaware. I started to thank him for letting me come but I realized that the words which came did not make sense. I began to cry, and heard my own voice repeating over and over and with agony, "They say I am against the Negro."

That accusation in the Party resolution had made me suffer more than all the other vilification and I, who had for years been regarded as a hard Communist, wept as I felt the sting anew.

Monsignor Sheen put his hand on my shoulder to comfort me. "Don't worry," he said. "This thing will pass," and he led me gently to a little chapel. We both knelt before a statue of Our Lady. I don't remember praying, but I do remember that the battle within me ceased, my tears were dried, and I was conscious of stillness and peace.

When we left the chapel Monsignor Sheen gave me a rosary. "I will be going to New York next winter," he said. "Come to me and I'll give you instructions in the Faith."

On my way to the airport I thought how much he understood. He knew that a nominal Christian with a memory of the Cross can easily be twisted to the purposes of evil by men who masquerade as saviors. I thought how communist leaders achieve their greatest strength and cleverest snare when they use the will to goodness of their members. They stir the emotions with phrases which are only a blurred picture of eternal truths.

In my rejection of the wisdom and truth which the Church has preserved, and which she has used to establish the harmony and order set forth by Christ, I had set myself adrift on an uncharted sea with no compass. I and others like me grasped with relief the fake certitude offered by the materialists and accepted this program which had been made even more attractive because they appealed for "sacrifice for our brothers." Meaningless and empty I learned are such phrases as "the brotherhood of man" unless they have the solid foundation of belief in God's Fatherhood.

When I left Monsignor Sheen I was filled with a sense

of peace and also with an inner excitement which stayed with me for many days. I flew back to New York late that night, a beautiful, moonlight night. The plane flew above a blanket of clouds, and over me were the bright stars. I had my hand in the pocket of my blue wool coat and it was closed over a string of beads with a cross at the end. All the way to New York I held tightly to the rosary Monsignor Sheen had given me.

For the rest of that year I remained alone in New York, limited in my contacts to the few clients I served and the occasional friend who dropped in. Now and then I stepped into a church to sit there and rest, for only there was the churning inside of me eased for a while and only then fear left me.

Christmas, 1950, was approaching, and again my loneliness was intensified. I was now living in a furnished room on Broadway at Seventy-fifth Street and still shuttling from my room to my office and back again every day and night.

On Christmas Eve, Clotilda and Jim McClure, who had lived at my house on Lexington Avenue and who had kept in touch with me and worried about me, called and urged me to spend the evening with them. After I sold my home they had had a miserable time finding accommodations. Harlem and its unspeakable housing situation was a cruel wilderness cheating the patient and undemanding. The McClures had moved to a one-room apartment on 118th Street where the rent of the decontrolled apartment was fantastic for what it offered. But Jim and Clo made no apologies for their home, for they knew how I grieved at their predicament.

It was cold when I arrived, but I forgot that in the warmth of their welcome. They rubbed my cold hands and put me in their one easy chair, and Clo served a simple supper. Jim said grace as he had always done at our house. We talked about Christmas, and as I listened to them I knew why bitterness had not twisted these two. They had made the best of what they had. They were gay and full of life, and above all they were touched with a deep spirituality which made their shabby room an island of harmony. There in a squalid building on an evil-looking street with its back areas cluttered with refuse and broken glass they had found spiritual comfort.

After we had eaten, Jim opened his well-worn Bible and read a few of the psalms and then Clo read several. As I listened to their warm, rich voices sounding the great phrases I saw that they were pouring their own present longings into these Songs of David, and I realized why the prayers of the Negro people are never saccharine or bitter. Jim handed me the book and said: "Here, woman, now you read us something."

I leafed through the pages until I found the one I wanted. I began to read the wonderful phrases of the Eighth Psalm:

"For I will behold the heavens, the works of Thy fingers . . . What is man that Thou art mindful of him? . . . Thou hast made him a little less than the angels . . . Thou hast subjected all things under his feet. . . . Lord, our Lord, how admirable is Thy name in all the earth."

For a few moments after I had finished no one spoke. I handed the Bible back to Jim. Clo poured another cup of coffee for me. Then I said I was tired and ought to get home since it was almost eleven o'clock. I promised I would come again soon, and Jim walked with me to the Madison Avenue bus and wished me a "Merry Christmas."

The bus was crowded with chattering and happy people. I sat alone in the midst of them, with my face against the window, watching the drab streets go by. On many of those corners I had campaigned. I had walked many of them in a succession of months of meaningless activity, a squandering of my creative years in sham battle. So many wasted years, I thought, drab as the streets!

So immersed was I in my thoughts that I forgot to get off the bus when it reached Seventy-second Street to transfer for the west side. I realized I had gone too far, but had no real desire to get off the bus at all, and I watched Madison Avenue turn from stores and flats into smart shops and hotels, and when we crossed Forty-second Street I still did not get off the bus.

I have no recollection of leaving the bus at Thirty-fourth Street or of walking along that street to the west side. My next recollection is of finding myself in a church. The church, I learned later, was St. Francis of Assisi.

It was crowded. Every seat was filled. There was hardly room to stand, for people packed the aisles. I found myself wedged in the crowd, halfway between the altar and the rear of the church.

Services had begun. From the choir came the hymns of Christmas. Three priests in white vestments took part in the ancient ritual. The bell rang three deep notes; the people were on their knees in adoration. I looked at the faces etched in the soft light, faces reverent and thankful.

It came to me as I stood there that here about me were the masses I had sought through the years, the people I loved and wanted to serve. Here was what I had sought so vainly in the Communist Party, the true brotherhood of all men. Here were men and women of all races and ages and social conditions cemented by their love for God. Here was a brotherhood of man with meaning.

Now I prayed. "God help me. God help me," I repeated over and over.

That night, after Midnight Mass was over, I walked the streets for hours before I returned to my rooming house. I noted no one of those who passed me. I was alone as I had been for so long. But within me was a warm glow of hope. I knew that I was traveling closer and closer to home, guided by the Star.

CHAPTER SEVENTEEN

EARLY IN THE NEW YEAR I went to the office of the Board of Education to see Dr. Jacob Greenberg, then superintendent in charge of personnel, regarding a teacher. In his office I met Mary Riley, his assistant. Since Dr. Greenberg could not see me at once, Miss Riley and I began to talk.

She had been a high-school teacher for years. Loved and respected by all, she represented a type of teacher becoming increasingly rare, as though they were being systematically eliminated from our schools. She was a woman of poise and dignity whose love of God permeated all her relations.

I felt relaxed as I sat there talking with her, listening to her and looking at the picture she made with her soft gray hair, her warm blue eyes, the quiet good taste of her dress. I was somewhat surprised that she would talk to me for I knew that my activities and the doctrine I had spread had been offensive to her. But she was smiling and saying she was sorry they no longer saw me at the Board. I explained that I had been having a lot of trouble.

She knew. "That's putting it mildly," she said. "But don't let anyone stop you, Bella. You still have a lot of friends. We don't like communism but we do admire one who struggles to help human beings as you always have."

I was moved by her words, for it was not the kind of talk I had heard of late. She went on to speak about the Interracial Council that she had founded in Brooklyn, and of which she was still a moving spirit. And I had a feeling that I was close to the edge of a new world, one in which acts of kindness were carried out anonymously and not used for publicity purposes. Some days later a package came from Mary Riley. It contained books and magazines dealing with a variety of things Catholic, such as the medical missions in Africa, the Interracial Councils, and youth shelters. There was also a book by a priest: James Keller's *You Can Change the World*.

As I read the title my thoughts went back to Sarah Parks, my teacher at Hunter College, and the books she had given me that had quickened my interest in the communist movement. Those books had been in praise of the change in the world brought about by the Russian Revolution which at the time I had considered an upheaval necessary for the improvement of the social conditions of the Russian people. I knew now that glorification of revolution and destruction of lives in the hope that a better world would rise were fatally wrong. I thought with sadness of Sarah Parks — her bright intelligence wasted because she had no standard to live by, of how in the end she took her own life rather than face its emptiness.

I thumbed through Father Keller's book. It was almost primitive in its simplicity and I was caught by its personal invitation to each reader — a call for self-regeneration. It seemed addressed to me personally. This was a new call to social action. This was no stirring of hate to bring about social reform but the stirring of the flame of love.

I could not stop reading the book. I sat there in the quiet of my office and I felt all through me the truth of Father Keller's saying: "There can be no social regeneration without a personal regeneration." As I read I felt life flowing back into me, life to myself as a person. Within the Party I had been obliterated except as part of the group. Now, like some Rip Van Winkle, I was awakening from a long sleep.

Father Keller did not leave me with a sense of aloneness or of futility. "It is better to light one candle than to curse the darkness," he had written. To me, who had begun to feel that evil was ready to envelop the world, this was life itself. I was grateful to Mary Riley and grateful to the priest for his words of life.

Not long afterward I was in the Criminal Courts Building defending a youthful offender and I ran into Judge Pagnucco, formerly of the District Attorney's office, who had interrogated me during the Scottoriggio investigation. We talked about the measure of individual responsibility for criminal acts. He mentioned Father Keller's words on that subject and I said I had heard of him and admired his work. The Judge asked me if I would like to meet the Maryknoll priest.

Next afternoon I met the Judge at the office of Godfrey Schmidt, a militant Catholic lawyer, and a teacher at Fordham Law School. I remembered him vividly as the official in the New York State Department of Labor who had prepared the case against Nancy Reed, the girl who had lived at my apartment for a time and whose mother was an owner of the *Daily Worker*. I thought of the violent campaign the Party had organized against him, the gruesome caricatures of him in the Party-controlled papers, and how they called him "Herr Doktor Schmidt." Now I listened to Godfrey Schmidt talk of America and its people with obvious sincerity, and I had an overwhelming feeling of shame that I had participated in that campaign of hate.

Father Keller came in with another friend and Mr. Schmidt invited us to lunch together. I looked at the priest in frank appraisal and found myself interested in the harmony and peace of his face and in his keen understanding of the problems facing men and women of our day. As he and the other men discussed various matters, I realized why these three talked so differently from the little groups I had been with at tables like this in the communist movement. Here there was no hatred and no fear. We talked of books and television and of communism too, and Father Keller referred to the latter as "the last stage of an ugly period."

When he invited me to his office to meet some of the Christophers I accepted. I found myself returning again and again to that office, impressed with the spiritual quality I found there. On my first visit to the Christopher headquarters a dozen of us were busy in the room when the chimes from the nearby Cathedral rang the noon hour. Everyone stopped working and recited the Angelus. I caught, here and there, remembered words of prayer I had heard long ago. ". . . Behold the handmaid of the Lord," I heard, and ". . . the Word was made flesh and dwelt among us."

I did not know the response and I stood silent. But I was deeply stirred to hear young men and women pausing in their work to pray together, here in the most materialistic city ever raised by a materialistic civilization. And I felt how true of this believing little group were the words: "And dwelt among us."

My association with the Christophers showed me how

little I knew of my Faith and made me realize that I was like a dry tinder box and that I wanted to learn. Seeing the Christophers at work stirred a memory of the flame I had in my youth, the desire to help those in trouble, the sense of shame at any indignity to a human being. I smiled ruefully in recalling that I had thought the Communists the modern prototype of the early Christians, come to cast greed and selfishness from the world. The Communists too had promised an order and a harmony of life. I knew now that their promises were fraudulent, and that the harmony they promised brought only chaos and death. Yet I knew too that I had to get the difference between the two clear in my own mind before I took any further steps. I had to know, and for myself.

I prayed now every day. I rose early in the morning and went to Mass at the Church of Our Lady of Guadaloupe, near where I now lived on West Seventeenth Street. I felt excitement when I turned east from Eighth Avenue and hurried up the church steps to hear the Brothers sing matins before Mass. As I watched the faces of the morning communicants, I envied them and longed to be one with them, and when each returned from the altar I felt a warm glow merely in being close to them. I thought of this continuous Sacrifice on the altars of thousands of churches all over the world, wherever there was a priest to bring the Mass to the people.

The anti-clericalism which had been a part of my thinking for years dropped from me completely when I watched the lights turned on each morning around the altar of Our Lady of Guadaloupe and when the candles were lighted and I saw the priest offer the Sacrifice. I felt myself inescapably drawn to the altar rail, but I still sat in the darkness of the rear pews as a spectator. I was not ready, I told myself. And I had a dread of dramatic gestures. But as

242

the days went by I knew the sense of strain was leaving me and I began to feel an inner quiet.

I found myself reading, like one who had been starved, books which the Communists and the sophisticated secular world marked taboo or sneered at. I found St. Augustine and the *City of God* infinitely more life-giving than the defiant modern professors who wrote *The City of Man*. I found St. Thomas Aquinas and I laughed to remember that all I had learned of St. Thomas was that he was a scholastic philosopher who believed in the deductive method of thinking. Now, as the great storehouse of his wisdom was opened to me, I felt rich beyond all words.

One day at lunch with Godfrey Schmidt I explained that I must learn more about the Faith. As we walked down Park Avenue, he took me into a bookshop and bought me a prayer book. Next day he called me to say that Bishop Sheen was in town and had agreed to see me again. This was like a joyful summons from an old friend.

With Mr. Schmidt I went to East Thirty-eighth Street, to the offices of the Society for the Propagation of the Faith, and rang the bell. Bishop Sheen opened the door himself and I saw the silver cross on his chest, the smile in his eyes, but this time I heard a welcome home in his greeting.

And so I began to receive instructions in the Faith. Something strange was apparent to me in my behavior — I who had generally been skeptical and argumentative now found that I asked few questions. I did not want to waste one precious moment. Week after week I listened to the patient telling of the story of God's love for man, and of man's longing for God. I listened to the keen logic and reasoning that have lighted the darkness and overcome the confused doubts of others of my group who had lost the art of reasoned thinking and in its place had put assertive casuistry. I saw how history and fact and logic were inherent in the foundations of the Christian faith.

I listened to the Bishop explaining the words of Jesus Christ, the founding of His Church, the Mystical Body. I felt close now to all who received Communion in all the churches of the world. And I felt the true equality which exists between people of different races and nations when they kneel together at the altar rail — equal before God. And I came to love this Church which made us one.

I read often long into the night. There were so many things I had to know. I had wasted so many precious years.

Easter of 1952 was approaching and Bishop Sheen said that I was ready. I had no baptismal record and a letter of inquiry to the town in Italy where I was born produced none, though I was reasonably certain I had been baptized. So it was decided I was to receive conditional baptism.

On April 7th, the anniversary of my mother's birthday, I was baptized by Bishop Sheen at the font in St. Patrick's Cathedral. Mary Riley and Louis Pagnucco stood on either side of me. Godfrey Schmidt and a few other friends were with me too.

Afterward Bishop Sheen heard my first confession. He had noted that I was nervous and distraught in making my preparation, for I had to cover the many years in which I had denied the truth. I meditated on the mockery I had made of my marriage; how I had squandered my birthright as a woman; on my twisted relationship with my parents; on the exaggerated pride of my mind; and on the tolerance I had for error. He realized my despair and said comfortingly: "We priests have heard the sins of men many times. Yours are no greater than those of others. Have confidence in God's mercy." After hearing my confession he granted absolution. His *Pax vobiscum* echoed and re-echoed in my heart.

At Mass next morning I received Communion from his hands. And I prayed as I watched the flicker of the sanctuary lamp that the Light that had reclaimed me might reach the ones I loved who still sit in darkness.

It was as if I had been ill for a long time and had awakened refreshed after the fever had gone. I went about my work with a calm that surprised me. I seemed to have acquired a new heart and a new conscience.

Outwardly my life was changed not at all. I still lived in a cold-water flat on a street of tenement houses, but now I could greet my neighbors with no feeling of fear or mistrust. I was never to be lonely again, and when I prayed there was always the Presence of Him I prayed to.

As order and peace of mind returned to my life I was able to face intelligently the difficult ordeal of appearing before governmental agencies and investigating committees. I dreaded hurting individuals who were perhaps as blind as I had been and who were still being used by the conspirators. I dreaded the campaign of personal abuse which would be renewed against me.

Now I formulated and tried to answer three critical questions: Does my country need the information I am called upon to give? Will I be scrupulous in telling the truth? Will I be acting without malice?

I knew that the information which I had might be of some help in protecting our people. I knew also that honest citizens of our country were uninformed about the nature of Marxism and I recognized now that in the best sense of the word to "inform" means to educate. As avenues of education are blocked and twisted into propaganda by the agents of this conspiracy, my country needed the information I had to give.

But I dreaded the ordeal of testifying, when letters, telephone calls, and post cards of abuse came to me after my first appearance before the Internal Security Committee of the Senate. There was one interesting turn to the abuse: the bulk of it was in biblical terms — "Judas Iscariot," "thirty pieces of silver," "dost thou betray" were the most common expressions used. Quite a few quoted from the Gospel of St. Matthew the words telling how Judas Iscariot hanged himself and the writers ended with the exhortation, "Go thou and do likewise."

Now I saw in true perspective the contribution that the teachers and the schools of America have made to its progress, just as I was sadly aware of the darker picture some of the educators and the educated among us have presented. Justice Jackson has said that it is the paradox of our times that we in modern society need to fear only the educated man. It is very true that what a man does with his knowledge is that which, in one sense, justifies or indicts that education. A glance at the brilliant scientists who served the Hitler regime, and the Soviet scholars who serve the Kremlin, a look at the men indicted for subversion in our own country — all lead us to re-estimate the role of education. We are told that all problems will be solved by more education. But the time has come to ask: "What kind of education?" "Education for what?" One thing has become transparently clear to me: rounded education includes training of the will as much as training of the mind; and mere accumulation of information, without a sound philosophy, is not education.

I saw how meaningless had been my own education, how like a cafeteria of knowledge, without purpose or balance. I was moved by emotion and my education failed to guide me in making sound personal and public decisions. It was not until I met the Communists that I had a standard to live by, and it took me years to find out it was a false standard.

Now I know that a philosophy and movement that devotes itself to improving the condition of the masses of our industrial society cannot be successful if it attempts to force man into the mold of materialism and to despiritualize him by catering only to that part of him which is of this earth. For no matter how often man denies the spirit he will in an unaccountable manner turn and reach out to the Eternal. A longing for God is as natural a heritage of the soul as the heartbeat is of the body. When man tries to repress it, his thinking can only lapse into chaos.

I know that man alone cannot create a heaven on earth. But I am still deeply concerned about my fellow man, and I feel impelled to do what I can against the inhumanity and injustices that threaten his well-being and security. I am aware, too, that if good men fail to so love one another that they will strike vigorously to eliminate social ills, they must be prepared to see the conspirators of revolution seize power by using social maladjustments as a pretext.

I believe that the primary requisite for a sober apprisal of the present challenge of communism is to face it with a clear understanding of what it is. But it cannot be fought in a negative manner. Man must be willing to combat false doctrine with the Truth, and to organize active agency with active agency. Above all there must be a new birth of those moral values that for the past two thousand years have made our civilization a life-giving force.

Today there are unmistakable signs about us that the tide is turning, in spite of the fact that we have been so strongly conditioned by materialism. The turn is so apparent that I, personally, am filled with hope where once

I despaired. Many of the molders of public opinion in our country are still geared to capitulation and compromise, but among the people the change is very clear.

As I have traveled about the country I have seen evidences of this. I have seen men and women determined to set principle above personal gain. I have seen fathers and mothers study the school problem to help education from contributing to the training of a fifth column for the enemy. I have seen housewives in Texas, after a hard day's work, sit down to a course of study on the Constitution of the United States, and I have heard them explain what they learned to their children, determined that they shall not be robbed of their heritage.

We have increasingly seen in our country the rise of social and civic harmony in communities peopled with those of different national, racial and religious backgrounds. The men and women in these communities have set their hearts and their wills against the insidious work of the Communists who seek to pit one against the other to provoke racial and religious conflict.

I have seen groups of workers in trade unions meet and pray together as they plan for the safety of their country. They are determined that the union which is necessary in their struggle for daily bread shall not be used as a mechanism for the seizure of power.

But it is among the young people that I find the most arresting signs of change. This despite the fact that the newspapers and magazines are replete with horror stories of the decadence and unbelievable cruelty and criminality of some of our youth.

I have talked with young men returning from World War II and Korea who have gone back to the little towns all over America determined to make of their homes a citadel of moral strength in the face of the forces that

248

promote the disintegration of family life. I have seen intelligent, well-educated young men and women band together and move into slum areas in our big industrial cities, dedicated to light the flame of love as neighbors and friends of the unfortunate.

I was invited one night to supper by the young people at Friendship House in New York City's Harlem. I found them outwardly not very different from those I had met in the communist movement. The difference was that they were dedicated to a belief in justice under God and therefore could not be used as puppets by men bent on achieving power. The difference, too, was in their relation with their neighbors and those they sought to help. In the communist movement I was conscious of the fact that we promised the material millennium to all who joined our cause. Here at Friendship House they kept before all the primacy of the spirit, and those who came to them were helped more effectively because of this.

In the colleges, we see signs of a new type of student. I have noticed a change in college religious societies which in my day were formal and social with only a gesture in recognition of God. There now emerges a new phenomenon. Students are beginning to realize that the training of the mind is of little value to man himself or to society unless it is placed in the framework of eternal truths. Once again we witness an insistence upon the union of knowledge of the things of the spirit with those of the world. There is a growing demand that they no longer be severed.

I was particularly struck with this new type of student one evening last year when I spoke at the University of Connecticut before the Newman Club. The Club, which was housed in the basement of the chapel, was alive with activity. It had a library and a social center, and it had the guidance of two priests trained to understand the dangers facing the young intellectual in a society steeped in paganism.

That evening I had stayed so late in answering questions that Father O'Brien asked three young men to drive me to the train in New London. As we rode through the Connecticut hills it began to snow. I asked the young man who was driving what he was going to do after graduation. "Serve Uncle Sam, I guess," he replied. In his voice was no bitterness, no resentment — and I thought with sudden sadness of his possible future and that of all our young people. Then one of the boys said quietly, "Why don't we say the rosary for peace?" He started the *Credo* and there in the darkness of that country road, with the soft snow falling, we said the rosary for peace.

I was aware as I rode home that night that men such as these can change the world for the better, so much were they filled with love, so selfless was their zeal. I know that even if the Communists were sincere in the glittering promises they make, they would be incapable of fulfilling them for they cannot create the kind of men needed for the task. Whatever apparent good the Communists have achieved has come through human beings who despite the harsh materialism taught them still retained a memory of God and who, even without realizing it, drew on the eternal standards of truth and justice. But their store of such men is dwindling, and in spite of their apparent victories men schooled in darkness are doomed to defeat.

New armies of men are rising, and these are sustained not by the Communist creed but by the credo of Christianity. And I am keenly conscious that only a generation of men so devoted to God that they will heed his command, "Love one another as I have loved you," can bring peace and order to our world.

INDEX

Abraham Lincoln Brigade, 88, 91–2, 188

Abraham Lincoln School, Chicago, 150

Abt, John, 194

Adams, Josephine Truslow, 114

Addams, Jane, 99

Albany, New York: author's work in, as legislative representative of Teachers Union, 77, 83 ff.; State Constitutional Convention of 1939, 112, 114; Communists in, 154, 161

Amalgamated Clothing Workers, 197

America, Russia and the Communist Party in the Post-War World, by Counts and Child, 134

American Association of University Teachers, 65

American Committee for Cultural Relations with Italy, 212

American Committee for Peace and Democracy, 125

American Federation of Labor, 76 ff., 105, 117, 121, 128

American Federation of Teachers, 57, 72, 99 ff., 117, 118, 127–8, 133–4, 158

American Labor Party, 78, 80–2, 106–7, 112–13, 115, 123, 127, 142–5, 168, 169, 176, 177, 197, 198, 203, 224

American Mobilization Committee, 125, 137

American Teacher, The, 100

Amter, Israel, 106, 120, 183, 190

Amtorg, 145

Anti-fascism, 67, 86–92

Anti-Fascist Literature Committee, 68

Artists, Scientists and Professionals, Independent Committee of, 176, 203

Associated Press, 220

Avialano, Italy, 3–9, 11, 13

Axtelle, George, 117

Babsky, Sid, 91

Backer, George, 113

Backman, Albert, 43

Beale, Fred, 158

Beard, Charles A., 38

Beethoven Hall, 78, 79

Berle, A. A., 41

Berlin, Germany, 53–4

Berti, Professor, 180–1

Bildersee, Dr. Adele, 25

Bill of Rights, 159

Birmingham, Stephen, 165

Bloor, "Mother," 185

Blumberg, Albert, 102, 203

Board of Education, New York: Class Room Teachers delegations to, 72; and substitute teachers, 110–12, 119; Communist fight against, 134

Boer, John de, 105

Borchard, Selma, 117

Bowery Savings Bank, 61, 85

Bretton Woods Conference, 183

British Labor Party, 82

Bromfield, Louis, 145

Brookings Institute, 39

Brooklyn, American Labor Party in, 143

Brooklyn Eagle, 1937 strike, 104

Browder, Earl: appearance and manner, 67–8; and Marxism, 95; heads Communist Party, 140; and Marcantonio, 141–2; attempt to Americanize Communist Party, 148–9, 162; prestige in national politics, 150, 154, 171; at meetings of Politburo, 163; at 1944 Party convention, 164; writes *Victory and After*, 169; break with Anna Damon, 172; calls for dissolution of Communist Party, 172–3; and re-election of Roosevelt, 173; forms Communist Political Association, 174; and concealed members of Party, 177; difficulties with Communist International, 181–2; accused of "revisionism," 182 ff.; trip to Moscow, 192; expelled from Party, 194

Browder, William, 210

Browderism, 180 ff., 189

Brownell, Herbert, 112

Bryce, Lord James, 38

Burlak, Ann, 185

Burlingame, Dr. Elizabeth, 25

Cahiers du communisme, 181

Call, The, Socialist publication, 22

Castle Hill, Westchester County, New York, 14

Catholic Church: and Spanish Civil War, 87–8; Bella Dodd's return to, 230 ff.

Cenacle of St. Regis, New York, 23

Central Trades and Labor Council of New York (A.F. of L.), 78, 79

"Chester," in charge of Communist Party Intelligence, 96, 122, 207, 208–9

Chicago Teachers Federation, 99–100

Chicago Teachers Union, 117

Childs, John, 117, 133–4, 176

Childs, Morris, 201

Christophers, the, 241–2

Church of Our Lady of Pompeii, New York, 131

Church of St. Lucy, East Harlem, 3

CIO, 104–6, 125, 128, 143

CIO Local 555, 147

CIO Political Action Committee, 176

City College, New York, 64, 128, 129, 130

City Hall, New York, 63, 77, 119, 192

City of God, by St. Augustine, 243

City of Man, The, 243

Class Room Teachers Association, 72–3

Clendenning, Dr., 16, 19

Clendenning, Gabrielle, 17

Coe, Charles, 176

Colligan, Dr. Eugene, president

of Hunter College, 63, 75, 108
Columbia University: summer session at, 33; graduate school, political science department, 38; courses at, 41; Teachers College, 42–3; author's degree from, 46. *See also* Teachers College
Cominform, 214–15
Comintern, Sixth World Congress of, 93
Committee on Economic Development, 210
Committee on Peace, 137
Committee to Defend the Public Schools, 120
Communism: as a philosophy, 39; in Germany, 53, 54; and Catholicism, 87–8
Communist Headquarters, New York, 67, 162–3
Communist International, 78, 88, 125, 171, 181–2, 183
Communist Party in U.S.: membership in, 41; dedication of early members of, 66 ff.; and funds for anti-fascist causes, 67; appeal to masses, 70–1; and A.F. of L., 76 ff.; and seamen's strikes, 78–9; attitude toward unions, 80; use of "fractions," 81; and A.F. of L., 82 ff.; night clubs financed by, 86, 209; and Spanish Civil War, 86–91; and Teachers Union, 93 ff.; influence among liberals and learned societies, 98; and American Federation of Teachers, 100–1; representation at teachers conventions, 105; and Rapp-Coudert investigation, 116 ff., 119 ff.,

134; loss of membership following Nazi-Soviet pact, 118; intelligence apparatus of, 122; pacifism of, at beginning of World War II, 125; swing to pro-war policy, 125, 134, 137, 139; and Schappes case, 129, 130; wartime activities, 137 ff., 148–9; change in public attitude toward, 138; espionage activities, 138; relationship of Vito Marcantonio to, 140–2; fight for control of American Labor Party, 142; Marxist schools, 148 ff., wartime control of workers, 152–4; and Soviet-American unity, 154–5; headquarters of, 162–3, 169, 213; Politburo, 163; dissolution of, 172 ff.; re-established as Communist Political Association, 172, 174; work for re-election of Roosevelt, 173 ff.; attempted Americanization of, 174; support of United Nations Charter, 178; change of direction and elimination of "Browderism," 180 ff.; re-established after dissolution of Communist Political Association, 190; expulsion of Browder, 194; and international peace movement, 194; expulsions from, 195 ff.; moves against Bella Dodd, 195–6; in 1946 elections, 197–9; propaganda to American Negroes, 200; and Progressive Party, 202–5; finances of, 208–11; Bella Dodd's expulsion from, 215–18
Communist Political Associa-

253

tion. *See* Communist Party, 173

Communists: at Hunter College, 28, 63–4, 71; regarded as advanced liberals, 38, 39; in Germany, 53–4; interest in New York, 71; school teachers, 65–6; asceticism of, 66–7; anti-fascist activities, 67–8; in Teachers Union, 72–3, 77; and Mayor LaGuardia, 106–7; use of grievances of substitute teachers, 110–12; and Soviet-Nazi pact, 118, 119; expelled from American Federation of Teachers, 127–8, 133

Conboy, Dr. John, 19

Condon, Dr., principal of Public School Number Twelve, 16

Congress, American, 45

Congress of American Women, 194–5

Congressional Directory, 45

Constitution, American, 38, 159, 248

Cooper, Bessie Dean, 42

Coudert, Frederic, 115, 119–20, 144–5

Counts, George: report on Russian education, 43, 58; opposition to Communist leadership in Teachers Union, and American Federation of Teachers, 117, 128; ideas and writings, 134; and Liberal Party, 176–7

Cracow, University of, 65

Crane, John, 212

Crimea Conference, 153

Curran, Joseph, 78–9, 165

Daily Worker, The, 94, 114,

125, 152, 162, 165, 183, 184, 201, 215, 220

Damon, Anna, 171–2

Darcy, Sam, 170–1

Davidson, Ben, 117

Davidson, Eve, 117

Davidson, Jo, 176

Davies, Ambassador Joseph, 226

Davis, Ben, 185–6, 189, 193, 213

Davis, Dr. George S., president of Hunter College, 62

Davis, Jerome, 102, 103, 105

Dawson, Dr. Edgar, 36, 37

Debs, Eugene, 205

DeLacy, Hugh, 105

Democratic Party, 105, 106, 107, 113, 124, 142, 177, 198, 210

Dennis, Eugene, 192, 193, 194, 201–3, 204, 205

Dewey, Dr. John, 41, 43, 46, 58

Dewey, Thomas, 107, 129, 205

Diamond, Max, 72

DiFalco, Judge Samuel, 48

Dimitroff, Georgi, 200

Dodd, Bella V.: born Maria Assunta Isabella Visono, in Picerno, Italy, 1, 3; childhood in Avialano, 3–9; comes to America, 10; early life in New York, 11–17; accident and hospitalization, 18–19; at Evander Childs High School, 21–24; student at Hunter College, 24 ff.; at Columbia University, 33, 38–9, 42–3; substitute teacher at Seward Park High School, 35–6; instructor in political science department Hunter College, 36 ff.; Teachers College, 42–3; M.A. Degree at Columbia,

46; at New York University Law School, 48–50; bar examination, 52, 57; trip to Europe, 52–7; joins Teachers Union, 58; clerkship in law office, 59; marriage to John Dodd, 59–61; return to Hunter College, 61 ff.; and Instructors Association at Hunter, 62, 65, 71–2; early associations with Communists, 66 ff.; and Class Room Teachers Association, 72–3; early status in relation to Communist Party, 74, 75; drafts teachers' tenure bill, 75–6; leaves of absence from Hunter, 77, 84; legislative representative of Teachers Union, 76 ff.; 93 ff.; delegate to A.F. of L. Central Trades and Labor Council of New York, 78–9; delegate to State Federation of Labor Convention at Syracuse, 80–1; relations with A.F. of L., 82 ff.; work for Loyalist Spain, 86–92; and American Federation of Teachers, 110 ff.; member committee to negotiate with Yale Corporation for reinstatement of Jerome Davis, 103; resignation from Hunter College, 108; fulltime employee of Teachers Union, 109 ff.; campaign in aid of substitute teachers, 110–12; nominee for Assembly of American Labor Party, 112–13; and Rapp-Coudert investigation, 115, 116, 119–128, 130, 134; leader of Women's Trade Union Committee for Peace, 126; divorce from John Dodd, 126, 161; work for organization of School of Democracy, 148–9; and Jefferson School of Social Research, 149–50; decision to become card-carrying Communist, 155–9; legislative representative of Communist Party for New York District, 159 ff.; at Party Headquarters, 162–3, 169; at meetings of Politburo, 163; establishes law-office for contacts with non-Communists, 164; open Party affiliation, 164, 167, 171; association with Nancy Reed, 165–6; activities in East Harlem, 167–8; supervises legislative work of unions, 169; member of National Committee of Communist Political Association, 173; continued work with Communist teachers, 174; in charge of political campaigns, 175–7, 191; work for re-election of Roosevelt, 175 ff.; speeches at Communist meetings in Middle West, 178; work with Communist Youth, 178; and "revisionism" in Communist Party, 183 ff.; clashes with Thompson, 192–3; and organization of Congress of American women, 194–5; Party moves against, 196, 216; charges against, 196; relinquishes position as legislative representative, 197; placed on Communist Party slate for attorney general in State elections, 197; election activities, 198–9; subpoenaed by New York County grand jury, 199; at National Committee meeting of June 1947, 200–3; work for Italian elections, 211; attempts to withdraw from Party, 212 ff.; appearance before Discipline Committee, 213–16; expulsion from Party, 215–20; reprisals against, 221 ff.; appearance before Tydings Committee, 226–7; return to Catholic Church, 230 ff.

Dodd, John, 52, 59–61, 113, 115–16, 126, 161

Donnini, Professor, 180–1

Douglas, Dorothy, 105

Dubinsky, David, 113,118, 142, 143, 174, 176, 192, 224

Duclos, Jacques, 181–2, 184, 189, 191, 200, 206, 229

Dumbarton Oaks Conference, 183

East Harlem, New York, 2, 14, 141, 143, 145, 167, 169

Edgerton, Dr., 34, 35

Egan, Hannah, 32, 33

Einstein, Albert, 65

Emergency Convention of Communist Party, 186, 188–90

Engels, Friedrich, writings of, 66, 151

England: socialists in, 64; alliance with U.S., 124; Communists in, 200

Erica Reed, 89–91

Europe, trip to, in 1930, 52 ff.

Evander Childs High School, 18, 21, 22, 24

Ex-Servicemen's League, 69

Fabians, 64, 173

Farmers Union, 176

Fascism, 54, 56, 57, 67, 68, 86–92, 134

Federal Bureau of Investigation, 231

Feldman, Beatrice, 46, 52, 55, 60, 131

Field, Frederick V., 211

Finkelstein, Dr. Louis and family, 46, 60

Finkelstein, Jerry, 144–5

First American Revolution, The, by Jack Hardy, 96

Fish, Hamilton, 175

Flynn, Elizabeth Gurley, 163, 178, 185, 187–8

Ford, James, 163, 189, 214

Fordham Hospital, 18

Fortas, Abe, 225

Foster, William Z., 72, 78, 80, 139, 157, 163, 171, 182, 183, 184, 187, 188, 189, 193, 194, 200, 201, 202, 204, 205

France: Communists in, 91, 171; alliance with U.S., 124

Franco, General Francisco, 87, 90

Franz Joseph, Emperor, 55

Fraternal Clubhouse, 189, 190

Freedom House, 174

Freiheit, Yiddish newspaper, 162

French Communist Party, 171, 181–2, 232

French Revolution, 28

Friends of the Free Public Schools, 116–17

Friends of the Soviet Union, 63

Friendship House, 249

Furriers Union, 184, 187

Gannet, Betty, 196

Garibaldi Branch of Communist Party, 168, 169

Garibaldi Brigade, Spanish Civil War, 91

Gastonia, N.C., textile strike in, 158, 172
Gates, John, 201, 202, 203
George Washington High School, 94
Germany: in World War I, 18; rising fascism in, 53–4; visit to southern, 57; communist propaganda against, 86; Nazi-Soviet pact, 118, 125, 142
Gerson, Si, 106, 155, 159, 197
Gimbel, Mrs. Elinor, 135–6, 137
Gold, Benjamin, 187
Goldstein, Gertrude, 33
Goldstein, Judge Jonah, 129
Goldstein, Ruth, 27, 33, 34, 38, 46, 48, 73
Goldway, David, 148, 212
Goodwin, Allen, 164
Googe, George, 117
Gottwald, Clement, 200
Grand Jury, New York County, 199
Greeley, Horace, 17
Green, Gil, New York State chairman of Communist Party, 155–6, 159, 163, 164, 167, 169–70, 175, 176, 182–3, 188, 192
Green, Senator, 226
Greenberg, Dr. Jacob, 238
Greenwich Village, 51, 112, 140, 144
Grossman, Mary Foley, 102
Gustaferro, Margaret, 38

Haberman, Philip, 119
Hague, International Court at the, 37
Hanley, John, 83
Hardy, Jack. See Zysman, Dale
Harlem Commission, Communist Party, 218–19
Hausborough, Roy, 196

Hawes, Elizabeth, 135
Hayes, Mrs. Arthur Garfield, 145
Hayes, Dr. Carleton J. H., 41
Healey, May Andres, 84
Hendley, Charles J., president of Teachers Union, 94, 97, 121, 160
Herndon Case, 172
Hickenlooper, Sen. B. B., 226, 227
Hickenbottom, Dean Annie, 25, 26, 32
Hillman, Sidney, 192
History of the Labor Movement, by Bimba, 66
Hitler, Adolf, 54, 87, 125
Holmes, Justice Oliver Wendell, 46
Holy Family Church, 15
Hook, Sidney, 65
"Horton." See Schappes, Morris U.
Hudson, Roy, 89, 105, 157, 172, 187, 210
Hunter College: student life at, 24 ff.; author's graduation from, 33; instructorship at, 36, 37, 48, 50; political science courses at, 39; students from, in Germany, 53; Communist students at, 10, 63–4; Instructors Association at, 62 ff., 71–2, 73, 76; author's leaves of absence from, 77, 84; author's resignation from, 108, 109
Huntingdon Library, 16

Infels, Helen, 65
In His Steps, by Charles Monroe Sheldon, 20
Institute of Pacific Affairs, 228

Instructors Association, 62 ff., 71–2, 73, 76
International Brigade, Spanish Civil War, 88, 91–2
International Court at The Hague, 37
International House, Columbia University, 43
International Labor Defense, 172
International Publishers, 149, 162
International Seamen's Union, 78–9
Interracial Council, 239
Isaacs, Stanley, 135
Italian Commission, American Communist Party, 180–1, 213
Italian Communist Party, 181, 208
Italy: author's early years in, 1–10; trip to, 1930, 55–7; fascists in, 87; elections of 1948, 208, 211–12

Jack, Hon. Hulan, 160
Jackson, Justice, 246
Jefferson School of Social Science, 65, 150–1, 152, 175, 213
Jenkins, Ruth, 116
Jewish Commission, Communist Party, 162
Jews: reaction to Nazi-Soviet pact, 118
John Adams School, Boston, 150
John Dewey Society, 41
Johns Hopkins University, 102, 203
Joint Committee of Teachers Organizations, 84
Jones, Philip, 164

Keller, Rev. James, 239–41

Kieran, Dr. John, president of Hunter College, 62–3
Korea, war in, 229
Kross, Judge Anna, 135, 160
Krumbein, Charles, 120, 172
Kuntz, Edmund, 130

La Follette, Robert, 205
Lagana, Tony, 198, 199
LaGuardia, Mayor Fiorello: city politics under, 63; helps author obtain leaves from Hunter, 84, 104; political methods of, 106–7; and Rapp-Coudert investigation, 115; attitude on teacher problems, 118–19, 134; and Vito Marcantonio, 141; support of Coudert, 145; Communists work for defeat of, 192
Lattimore, Professor Owen, 225–6
Lautner, John, 219–20
Lawrence, William, 189
League against War and Fascism, 125
League for Industrial Democracy, 64
League of Nations, 37
Lefkowitz, Dr. Abraham, Teachers Union leader, 72, 83, 94, 95, 117, 128
Lehman, Governor Herbert, 76, 112
Lenin, V. I.: teachings of, 66, 67, 80, 95, 104, 140, 148, 151, 169, 173, 181, 187
Leslie, Kenneth, 135
Levine, Morris, 36
Lewis, Celia, 72, 96, 97
Lewis, John L., 104, 157–8
Lewis, Ted, 165–6
Liberal Party, 117, 176–7
Liberals, 98

Lincoln, Abraham, 136
Linville, Dr., Teachers Union leader, 72, 94, 95
Lippman, Walter, 174
Lodge, Senator Henry Cabot, 226
London School of Economics, 39
Lovestonites, 117, 120, 128
Loyalists. *See* Spanish Civil War
Lugano, Italy, 1
Lynch, Helen, 71
Lyons, Thomas, 121

McCarthy, Senator Joseph, 225, 226
McClure, Clotilda, 167–8, 234–5
McClure, James, 167–8, 234–5
McGrath, Congressman Christopher, 75, 230–32
McHenry, Beth, 165
McKenney, Ruth, 195
McMahon, Senator Bryan, 226
Madison Square Garden rallies, 154–5
Madison, Wisconsin, American Federation of Teachers convention in, 104–5, 128
Mann, Allie, 102
Marcantonio, Vito: political heir of LaGuardia, 106; relationship of, to Communist Party, 140–2, 168; 1942 campaign for Congress, 143–4; and campaign of Jerry Finkelstein for State Senate, 145; activities of, 168–9; and Anna Damon, 172; and 1946 elections, 197–9
Marsica, Fidelia, 3
Marsica, Maria Antonia, 3
Marsica, Severio, 3

Martha Berry Schools, 64
Marty, André, 91
Marx, Karl, writings of, 66, 95, 151, 187
Marxism, 27, 30, 74, 80, 95, 98, 104, 148, 181
May Day parades, 85–6, 104
Means, Gardiner, 41
Meany, George, 78, 113
Medina, Judge Harold, 52
Midol, Lucien, 170
Mindel, "Pop," 214, 215, 229
Miners Union, 157
Minor, Robert, 163, 172
Minton, Bruce, 195
Mission to Moscow, by Joseph Davies, 226
Missouri v. Holland decision, 39
Mitchell, MacNeil, 113
Moley, Raymond, 39
Molotov, V. M., 87, 118
Morris, Robert, 119, 226
Mt. Kisco, New York, 29
Mulzac, Captain, 166
Munn, Misses, 14, 20
Murray, Philip, 158
Myers, Blackie, 78–9, 165

Naples, Italy, 10, 57
Nation, The, 29
National Association of Manufacturers (NAM), 175
National Board of Communist Party, 174, 175, 182, 187, 192, 194. *See also* Politburo
National Citizens Political Action Committee, 177
National Committee of Communist Party, 184–7, 190, 199–203
National Education Association (NEA), 175
National Maritime Union, 88, 89, 165, 166

259

National Socialism, 53–4
Naturalists' Club, 21
Nazis, 54, 118, 139
Negroes: wartime demands opposed by Communists, 153; and Communist Party in South, 185; on National Committee of Party, 186; on National Board, 189; Bella Dodd accused of "white chauvinism," 196, 217; communist line to Southern, 200; resistance to communism, 200
Newark Ledger, 1937 strike, 104
Newman Club: Hunter College, 26, 32; University of Connecticut, 249
New Republic, The, 28
New York Bar, 52
New York City, 1–2, 11 ff.; and mayoralty of LaGuardia, 63; situation of teachers in, 65; 1937 elections, 106–7
New York County Grand Jury, 199
New York Post, 113, 223
New York State Constitutional Convention, 112
New York State Department of Education, 135
New York State Labor Department, 165, 240
New York University, 65
New York University Law School, 48 ff.
"Nineteen Fivers," 95, 148
Norman, William, 196, 209
North American Committee for Loyalist Spain, 89, 91

O'Connell, Genevieve, 23
O'Connor, Tom, labor editor of *P. M.,* 146

O'Dwyer, William, 191–2
Odessa, Russia, 91
Oumansky, Constantine, Soviet Ambassador to the U.S., 183
Our Lady of Guadalupe Church, 241–2

Pagnucco, Judge Louis, 240, 244
Parent Teachers Association, 77
Parks, Sarah, 25, 26, 28, 30, 50, 51, 239
Patterson, William, 186
Pearl Harbor, 136
Pen and Hammer, 129
Pennypacker, Annie, 114
Perry, Pettis, 186, 188
Philadelphia, American Federation of Teachers convention in, 101
Picerno, Italy, 1, 2, 3
P. M., 146
Poletti, Charles, 112
Politburo, 139, 140, 163, 170, 171, 172, 174
Potash, Irving, 184
Potenza, Italy, 1, 2, 7, 10
Poughkeepsie, N. Y., 114, 115, 131
Progressive Businessmen's Committee, 210
Progressive Education Association, 41
Progressive Party, 123, 204–5
Progressive Republicans, 124
Protestant, The, 135
Public School Number One, 13
Public School Number Twelve, 16, 18
Puerto Ricans, 144, 167, 217

Quill, Michael, 193
Quinn, Michael, 125

Rapp-Coudert investigation,

115, 119 ff., 128, 129, 130, 134, 148, 226
Rapp, Herbert, 115, 119
Reed, Ferdinanda, 114, 165
Reed, Nancy, 165, 240
Rees, Mina, 32
Republican Party, 106, 107, 113, 142, 197, 198, 210
"Revisionism," in Communist Party, 180 ff.
Ribbentrop, Joachim von, 87, 118
Rieber, Clara, 72, 96, 97
Riley, Mary, 238–9, 240, 244
Roe, Wellington, 224–5, 226
Rogan, John, 166
Rogers, Dr. Lindsey, 39
Rome, 56–7
Roosevelt, Mrs. Eleanor, 127
Roosevelt, President Franklin D., 63, 81, 151, 157, 171, 173, ff., 175, 176, 177
Rose, Alex, 113, 118, 142, 176
Rosenberg, Julius, 130
Russell, Rose, 159, 160, 161, 220
Russell Sage Foundation, 114
Russia, 43. *See also* Soviet Union
Russian Institute, 154, 226
Russian Revolution, 28, 51, 95, 239
Russian War Relief, 154
Ruthenberg, Charles, 172
Ryan, Joseph, 78, 79

St. Francis Hospital, Bronx, N. Y., 34
St. Francis Hospital, Poughkeepsie, N. Y., 115
St. Francis of Assisi Church, New York, 236–7
St. Peter's Episcopal Church, 16

St. Raymond's Church, 15
San Antonio, Texas, 99
San Francisco Conference, 179
Schappes, Morris U., 128–30
Schappes, Sonia, 128, 129
Schiff, Dorothy, 113
Schlauch, Dr. Margaret, 65–6, 67, 68, 160
Schmidt, Godfrey P., 165, 240–1, 243, 244
School for Democracy, 148 ff.
Schroon Lake, New York, 46
Scottoriggio, 198, 199, 240
Scottsboro Case, 66, 172
Scripps-Howard press, 181
Seamen's strikes, 78–9
Selsam, Howard: head Jefferson School of Social Science, 65, director School for Democracy, 148
Senate Internal Security Committee, 220, 246
Seward Park High School, 35, 36
Sheen, Rt. Rev. Fulton J., 231–4, 243–5
Sheldon, Charles Monroe, 20
Sherman, General William T., 60
Shiloh, battle of, 60
Silverman, Harriet, 66 ff., 74–5, 139, 156
Smith, Ferdinand, 166
Smith, Jessica, 194
Social Democrats, 142, 143, 174
Socialists: German, 53; English, 64; American, 100; in Teachers Union, 120; reaction to death of Trotsky, 128
Sororities, 32
Southern Committee for Human Rights, 185
Soviet-Nazi pact, 118, 125, 142
Soviet Union, 114; recognition

of, 1932, 63; and Germany, in World War II, 87; and Spanish Civil War, 89; socialism in, 95; Soviet-Nazi pact, 118, 125; war with Germany, 134; American aid to, 137–8; attitude of American Communists toward, 139; Communists work for Soviet-American unity, 169–70; Roosevelt's commitments to, 173; open support of Browder policy, 183; Browder visit to, 185, 192; imposes new line on American Communists, 192–3; and peace movement, 194; co-existence with, 276

Spanish Civil War, 86–91, 188, 189

Spellman, Francis Cardinal, 193, 215

Spellman, Howard Hilton, 59

Stachel, Jack, 80, 120, 139, 163

Stalin, Joseph, 188: writings of, 66, 95, 139, 187; dissolution of Communist International, 155; and "revisionism" in American Communist Party, 183

State County and Municipal Workers, 147

State Employment Bureau, 165

State Federation of Labor, 80–1

Student Council, Hunter College, 31, 32

Syracuse, New York, 80

Tammany Hall, 141

Teachers and labor, affiliation of, 99–106

Teachers College, Columbia University, 42, 43, 117

Teachers Guild, 128

Teachers Union: Bella Dodd's first contact with, 57–8; Class Room Teachers attacks on, 72; early communist minority in, 72–3; legislative work of, 76 ff.; need of A.F. of L. support, 82; and tenure law, 82–3; use of, by Communist Party, 83; and Spanish Civil War, 89; growth of communist fraction in, 93 ff.; author full-time employee of, 109 ff.; campaign in aid of substitute teachers, 110–12; build up of Communist Party leadership in, 112; fight against cut in State aid to education, 115; attempt to take leadership in, from Communists, 117; and Rapp-Coudert investigation, 120 ff.; end of formal relations with A.F. of L., 128, 133; proposal for nursery schools, 135; activities of members in behalf of Marcantonio, 144; support of Finkelstein, 144; affiliation with CIO, 147; headquarters in Tom Mooney Hall, 148; and School for Democracy, 148; author succeeded by Rose Russell in, 159; employment bureau of, 165; proposed affiliation with NEA, 175

Teachers Union Local Five, 72, 76, 93, 101, 120, 147

Teachers Union of Atlanta, 117

Teheran Conference, 153, 169, 170, 178, 181, 183

Tenth Assembly District, New York, 112–13, 144

Tenure bill for teachers, 75–6, 82–3

Third All-Russian Congress of the Russian Young Communist League, 140
Thomas Aquinas, St., 243
Thomas Paine School, New Rochelle, 150
Thompson, Robert, 91, 187, 188, 189, 192, 193, 196–7, 209, 213, 215, 220
Thorez, Maurice, 232
Tito, Marshal, 91
Tocqueville, Alexis de, 38
Togliatti, Palmiro, 200
Tom Mooney Hall, 147
Trachtenberg, Alexander, 149, 150, 188, 214–16
Trade Union Unity League, 72
Trotsky, Leon, 128
Trotskyites, 120, 128
Tuohy, Patrick, 186
TUUL, combine of Communist unions, 78
Tydings, Senator Millard, 226–7
Tydings Committee, 226–7

Unemployed councils, 69, 71
Unger, Abe, 107
United Nations Charter, 179
United States: World War II, 124, 137
United States Senate: treaty-making powers of, 39
Universal military training, 179
University of Berlin, 53
University of Connecticut, 249–50
USSR. *See* Soviet Union

Van Kleek, Mary, 114
Vassar College, 32
Vatican, visit to, 57
Victory and After, by Earl Browder, 169

Vienna, Austria, 55
Visono, Caterina, 12, 13, 14, 20
Visono, Rocco, 1–2, 61, 113, 115–16
Visono, Teresa Marsica, 1–3, 6–10, 11–14, 15–17, 18, 19, 20, 21, 113, 126, 130–1
Volume Library, 29

Wallace, Henry, 203, 204–5
Wallas, Dorothy, 94, 96–7, 121
Wardlaw, Ralph, 91
Warehousemen's Union, 147
Washington, D.C., 77, 154, 203
Weinfeld, Judge Edward, 112
Welles, Sumner, 154
Wesley, John, 20
Westchester County, New York, 14, 29
Whalen, Paddy, 69–71, 166
Whitman, Charles S., 119
Whitney, Anita, 165
Wiener, William, 156, 210–11
Willkie Memorial. *See* Freedom House
Willkie, Wendell L., 157
Williamson, John, 163
Wilson, President Woodrow, 37
Women's Trade Union Committee for Peace, 126, 139
Woodruff, Susan, 113–14, 165
Workers' Bookshop, 162
Workers School, 148, 149
World Telegram, New York, 181
World War I, 18, 41, 61
World War II, 70–1, 124, 137
Wortis, Rose, 105, 139, 156, 159
WPA: teachers in, 77, 84, 102, 104, 110–11; nursery school program, 135
WPA Local Number 453, 93

263

Yale Corporation, 103
Yale Divinity School, 102
Yalta Conference, 152, 179, 183
Yonkers, Communists in, 194

Young Communist League, 64, 71, 188

Zysman, Dale, vice president of Teachers Union, 96–7, 133–4

Made in the USA
Middletown, DE
09 August 2020